T0209301

THROUGH MY TEARS CAME

MIDNIGHT MEDITATION

DR. BARBARA BUTTERFIELD-JERVIS

THROUGH MY TEARS CAME MIDNIGHT MEDITATION

iUniverse books may be ordered through booksellers or by contacting:

iUniverse
1663 Liberty Drive
Bloomington, IN 47403
www.iuniverse.com
844-349-9409

Because of the dynamic nature of the Internet, any web addresses or links contained in this book may have changed since publication and may no longer be valid. The views expressed in this work are solely those of the author and do not necessarily reflect the views of the publisher, and the publisher hereby disclaims any responsibility for them.

Any people depicted in stock imagery provided by Getty Images are models, and such images are being used for illustrative purposes only.
Certain stock imagery © Getty Images.

Scripture quotations are from the Holy Bible, King James Version (Authorized Version). First published in 1611. Quoted from the KJV Classic Reference Bible, Copyright © 1983 by The Zondervan Corporation

ISBN: 978-1-6632-4238-9 (sc)
ISBN: 978-1-6632-4237-2 (e)

Library of Congress Control Number: 2022912744

Print information available on the last page.

iUniverse rev. date: 08/02/2022

Foreword

It has been my pleasure to have known and to have built an unbreakable bond with Dr Butterfield-Jervis since 1990. She's my mom. Through the years, I've watched my mother bear many struggles, and with the help of God through prayer and fasting, she overcame every time! My mom is a warrior who has fought for her happiness. I'm very proud of her for her commitment to God, her strength, her tenacity, and her integrity.

It's been a long time coming, but this book is finally here. I encourage you the reader to dive deep into each page and hold tight to the portions that are meant for you. I have no doubt that this book will be a blessing to you.

Mommy, you have gone through so much. You endured labour, raised me, and put your dreams on hold, putting me before yourself. How can anyone be so selfless? I cannot thank you enough. Congratulations on this masterpiece!

With love,

Tarina Parker

Introduction

We often speak of what we are going through, but the good news is that when we are going through difficult times, we are not stuck in our troubles with no way out. God never promises us trouble-free lives, but He does promise to be with us and to never leave us or forsake us. When God takes us through something, He will always teach us valuable lessons that we can use in the future.

Most of my life I've had hardships, but there were a few years of my life that were very challenging. The challenges I have overcome have taught me to look at obstacles in a different way.

During that time, I walked down a very lonely and dark path, and the only One I can give the praise to for bringing me through it is God.

One of the most important times to hear from God is when we need direction as we go through difficulties. What should we do? How long will the problem last? Trusting God to help us will keep us from giving up in the midst of our difficulties.

Challenges are what make life interesting. Overcoming them is what makes life meaningful. Obstacles are problems given to us humans to solve. It could be something as big as being born with a disability or something as simple as learning how to ride a bike. For me, it was going through a divorce as a Christian and a pastor.

I spent many nights lying awake all through the night, weeping as I thought about all that I was going through. I tried my best to save twenty-three-plus years of my life, but the decision was not totally up to me. As a result of that, I had to accept what was requested of me.

Amidst the nights of pain in my heart, my mind, and my soul, the only thing I accomplished was to have wet my pillow with the tears I cried. Sleep was far from me. I needed some relief from the grief I was carrying.

Living in a small community where almost everyone knew everyone else, I was judged, gossiped about, and criticized. I was made to feel as if I was the one who had asked for the divorce and that I was the one who was at fault.

There was no way to explain myself to anyone. Those who were willing to lend an ear were the ones who listened to me and prayed for me.

My mind began to play tricks on me, and I began to fall back into a state I had been in during my younger years: having a low self-esteem, not loving myself, and having thoughts of ending my life. Then one day a friend of mine told me to use those nights of no sleep to read more of the Word of God. From that night on, I began meditating and listening to gospel music that lifted my spirit. At one point I played an audio Bible whilst asleep to get my mind regulated spiritually.

Through that, I began to write what I called Midnight Meditations, and I started posting these on my Facebook page each night. The response to these posts eventually were overwhelming, and it encouraged me and motivated me to write more.

I used the pain that I was suffering to birth, or I should say bring back to life, my writing gift.

Through this whole experience, I regained my confidence. I was able to face whatever was out there for me to face. I had worn a mask throughout my entire life, so it was not hard for me to face things. I went through each day hiding all the pain I was feeling inside.

My other book, which I wrote a few years ago but never published, outlines most of what I had gone through from the time of being a child through to my adult life. Through God's grace, the prayers of a few friends, and the support of my daughter, I made it through this period of divorce.

Overcoming obstacles is never easy to begin with. Most obstacles are extremely hard and challenging. But by overcoming them, we get to know why they are important. The importance of overcoming obstacles in life is to make us braver, stronger, and wiser. And I can truly say that I am now all three. Everyone has their own obstacles to overcome, and some such obstacles are illustrated by my own experience

In any circumstance, the reality remains that we will always face challenges. Either we let those trials and problems get the best of us, or we decide to beat them by honing the right skills that will put those challenges to shame. Because at the end of the day, it's just a matter of how we respond to challenges that come our way.

For me, at the end of the day, if I don't see things through the eyes of an optimistic, hopeful, and able individual, then I am the only person who's going to lose.

When you let challenges get the best of you, there's no one to blame but yourself. And there's no one who's going to suffer the consequences but you.

Challenges, no matter your lot in life, are going to be a part of living. Everyone bumps into them at some point. And most, if not all, great achievements often arise from your turning those challenges into the opportunities of a lifetime.

Out of my nights of agony and tears, I present to you a collection of my writings which I have called *Through My Tears Came Midnight Meditation.*

Healing of Spiritual Wounds

As I reflect tonight, my mind goes to so many people who are going through difficult times, so many who are in need of healing. I am not talking about physical healing, although, yes, there are many who are in need of physical healing. No, I am speaking of spiritual woundedness. May I remind you that the spirit can be wounded just like the physical body can be wounded? If you have a broken leg, it will affect your comfort level, your mobility, your activity level, and many other aspects of your life. In much the same way, a spiritual wound will also affect these things.

So many people are trying to desperately hold on to God with wounded spirits. Sad to say, there are many who are discouraged by the wounds that were inflicted on them by the people who should have been administering healing to them. Yes, this is real. It is prevalent today more than ever before as we are nearing the return of the Lord.

The people we are closest to have the potential to wound us the most spiritually. You see, it is the people around whom we let our guard down who have the greatest ability to hurt us. When we are wary of someone, we close up, and when we trust someone, we open up. We let our guards down around people we trust. Thus, they are able to sometimes smite us below the fifth rib, in the deepest part of our beings, wounding us spiritually.

Proverbs 18:14 tells us, "A man's spirit sustains him in sickness, but a crushed spirit who can bear?" The physical body and the spirit are two different things. The spirit will pick you up when your body is down. If your spirit is wounded and you are suffering a serious sickness, then you have a double whammy. Not only are you physically sick, but also your spiritual side isn't functioning properly to encourage you in the Lord in terms of your suffering. You may start wishing to die or begin thinking about suicide, which can affect your ability to cope, to trust God, and to believe in Him for healing. It will affect you in many ways.

Tonight, let us be reminded that we have a God who is right there waiting for us to cast our cares on Him because He cares for us! He says that His yoke is easy and His burden is light!

Matthew 10:29–31 says, "Are not two sparrows sold for a farthing? And one of them shall not fall on the ground without your Father. But the very hairs of your head are all numbered. Fear ye not therefore, ye are of more value than many sparrows."

Sometimes just a reminder from God that He knows what we are going through is all we need to keep on keeping on. To hear of His concern for birds out in the middle of nowhere and that we are of more value than many birds is quite the balm for our wounded souls.

Let us go to bed with the assurance that God loves us, that He knows everything we are going through, and that there is a balm in Gilead to heal us! In the midst of it all, let us encourage ourselves in the Lord and allow Him to fix what needs to be fixed in our lives. Have a restful night!

Don't Drop out of the Race

But they that wait upon the Lord shall renew their strength; they shall mount up with wings as eagles; they shall run, and not be weary, they shall walk, and not faint. (Isaiah 40:31)

*D*uring a long race, it's easy to get discouraged. But what most runners know is that being familiar with the course helps you to keep up momentum and motivation. When you know what to expect, you are able to pace yourself and not get discouraged when the road seems endless.

God doesn't map out for us the exact course of our lives. But there are some things we can know without a shadow of a doubt. For example, we know troubles will come.

Each day we are faced with troubles and trials on this journey called life, especially those who are professed Christians. The Enemy sets out every day to tempt us, discourage us, and make us feel that there is no sense in serving God. He wants to see us fail. He wants to see us stop serving God.

We know and must be assured that God will never abandon us. We know that He has good plans for us. And we know that He will ultimately overcome evil in the world. In the end, God will win. The knowledge of His Word and our faith helps us persevere when the going gets tough and the race gets long. We can pray and ask God to give us greater confidence in Him so that we might persevere in the race of life, because this race is a hard one.

So no matter what may be weighing you down tonight, please know that God will give you the strength to endure and to come through as pure gold, victoriously. Have a good night's rest as you give all your problems over to the Great I Am, who never sleeps or slumbers and who is always working on our behalf. Have a blessed night!

Put It in God's Hand

And in that day ye shall ask me nothing. Verily, verily, I say unto you, Whatsoever ye shall ask the Father in my name, he will give it you. Hitherto have ye asked nothing in my name: ask, and ye shall receive, that your joy may be full. (John 16:23–24)

As children of God, we live in a world where we are ostracized on a daily basis. At our jobs, many of us are treated badly by bosses and supervisors, who tend make us feel depressed and discouraged, which causes us to wonder if we are who God says we are in the Bible.

Many cries goes out daily from those who are treated badly in their homes, amongst family members. There are those who are overlooked for promotions, and there are also those who are sick in their bodies with seemingly no end to their suffering.

Many people lie in bed at night thinking about the things they are faced with every day. They toss and turn all night. Then there are those who go to bed with heavy hearts.

There are times in our lives when we are going through tough times, so we tend to forget to pray, to seek counsel from God's Word. The Word of God admonishes us to pray about all things, not some things—and not just when everything is going well. Every so often we tend to forget to pray and read the Word of God when we face trials. Instead, we talk about and focus on the problem we are faced with.

I am here to remind you that no matter what you're going through, there is counsel in the Word of God for every situation you may be faced with. The Word says, "Many are the afflictions of the righteous, but God delivers them out of them all" (Psalm 34:19).

You may be reading this and saying to yourself, *When will He deliver? How long will I have to go through this?* May I ask you: have you told God about your situation? Your answer may be, "He is all-knowing, and He knows what I'm going through." Yes, He is all-knowing, but His Word tells us in John 16 that we are to ask. But ask what? Anything. Ask anything in His name, and He will do it. Just ask in the name of Jesus.

There are people who are at their wits' end and want to give up on life. You don't have to be one of those people. There is a solution. Jesus is the answer. He came to give you life and that more abundantly.

Give your situation to God. Wait patiently on Him. He may not come when you want Him to, but I can assure you tonight that He is always right on time! Give God all your requests, then rest peacefully tonight knowing that there is nothing too hard for Him to do. Have a restful night!

The Will of God

In everything give thanks; for this is the will of God
in Christ Jesus concerning you. (1 Thessalonians 5:18)

As I lie here tonight and reflect on my own life, I find that there's
a lot I can give God thanks for despite all that I have being
going through all my life. I thank God for all that He has brought
me through and continues to bring me through. I am thinking about
my book I am yet to publish entitled *My Pathway to Purpose*, which
highlights the path that I have trod in order to get where God wants
me to be—His will for my life!

I used to pray to God asking Him to stop the storms I was faced
with, but I don't pray that way anymore, because I have come to realize
that there are times when God allows storms in my life to get me where
I need to be.

I know that He is with me despite my moments of feeling as if
He's not there. He is there. There are times I hear His voice, and there
are times He is silent. In those moments of silence, He is carrying me
through the worst moments in my life. I have this assurance because
He cannot go back on His Word that says, "I will never leave you nor
forsake you!"

I want to say to you tonight that there is a ray of sunshine right behind the cloud. This experience is preparing you to occupy the kingdom. Out of this, He is preparing you to take your rightful place in the kingdom. So no matter what your circumstance is, God is going to give you beauty for ashes!

If you are faced with a storm in your life, don't give up and don't lose heart. God is preparing you for something great! When you come out of what you are going through, you will be greater, stronger, wiser, and better. Be encouraged that your greater days are just around the corner.

Like Job, let us wait until our change comes; it is on its way! Let's not give up! Have a safe and restful night.

You Were Created to Be Great

Come now, and let us reason together, says the Lord:
though your sins be as scarlet, they shall be as white
as snow; though they be red like crimson, they shall
be as wool. (Isaiah 1:18)

*M*any people go through life with questions, and when those
questions are not answered, it can leave room for confusion and
misunderstanding. For example, the Bible says, "The Lord will make
you the head and not the tail" (Deuteronomy 28:13), yet many people
spend much of their lives trying to prove that they are the tail.

Despite this scripture, there are many of us who feel as if this will
never happen. We will always be the tail in various aspects of our lives.
We will always be told and made to feel as if we are below.

Ironically, though, there is something about the human mind that
fights against accepting the idea of being the head. Many people find
it easy to listen to someone tell them they are not great, but they will
fight with the one who says, "There is so much more to you than what

you see!" If you are used to going through life with a foot on your neck, then believing that you are the head can be a challenge.

I want to tell you tonight that you were not created to be a doormat, to be walked on or discounted by anyone. Your silence may be the reason why people perceive you as weak. Did you know that the Enemy plants little suggestions to make you believe that as a follower of Christ you should just turn the other cheek and ignore what is happening to you?

Whoever you are, know that God never created you to be a doormat or a sponge that soaks up negativity. In fact, you were created to have dominion over the earth. Your problems should never tell you how to feel or what to do. You are supposed to tell your problems how they will make you feel.

As long as you remain silent and continue to allow yourself to shrink, you will never discover the true power that lives inside you! Have a blessed night.

Don't Look Back

I want to let you know tonight that just because you have made some mistakes in your past does not mean you should feel humiliated. You are not the first person to struggle with making the right decisions. You are not the only person to wake up in the morning saying, "I just don't feel like myself today."

One of the things I love about God is that He gives us opportunities to work out our own souls' salvation. Situations will always show up to challenge us to quit, but the Spirit is saying that regardless of what happens, always look for something bigger than ourselves. We mustn't settle for what we see in front of us. Life does get better than this. When we commit to doing the work, we will experience favourable results. Knowing who we are is key to building a legacy that will stand the test of time.

This season of your life has been very challenging. You may have been struggling to identify who you are. The people in your inner circle have conflicting opinions about who you really are. Believe it or not, some people in your inner circle do not believe who God says you are. You are at a crucial point in your life. The only reason you are facing opposition at this time is because you are about to walk into the hundredfold blessing that will change your life forever! Don't allow your past to deter you.

I can assure you that by the time the Holy Spirit is finished revealing Himself to you and through you, people will call you blessed and highly favoured and will see in you a true depiction of faith in action.

If you want to leave a legacy that has lasting effects, you have to make some major sacrifices. Your family or friends may never fully understand your actions, but you know there is a great call on your life and that it must be fulfilled. Years ago you made the choice to stop flying with eagles and started hanging with the chickens. Don't get stuck in the chickens' world, because the hundredfold blessing is about to overtake your life.

Allow everything from your past to be an afterthought. Don't get trapped in the lies of the Enemy. Open your eyes to see the full picture of God's promises. Don't allow people to judge you by the car you drive or the place you live. There is more to you than meets the eye.

Have a blessed night!

It Will Be Worth It All

And then shall they see the Son of man coming in the clouds with great power and glory. And then shall he send his angels, and shall gather together his elect from the four winds, from the uttermost part of the earth to the uttermost part of heaven. (Mark 13:26–27)

When we think about everything we go through here on earth, we may find it somewhat discouraging. We may get depressed and want to give up on life because of the struggle. May I say, the struggle is real, but nothing can be compared to what God has in store for us who love Him.

Giving up on life is the first thing the Enemy brings to you. And if you listen to him, you'll do just that. Whatever you are going through, God promises to give you the strength to endure it. He allows you to go through certain situations to refine you. He allows you to go through because He knows you will endure.

When Jesus was here on earth, He was human just as we are, and He suffered pain, criticism, loneliness, heartache, rejection, and ridicule just like we do. He knows first-hand how we feel—and that is why He is able to comfort us like nobody else can comfort us.

Our families, friends, and loved ones can comfort and encourage us, but only Jesus, our beautiful Saviour, can see into our hearts and literally feel our pain, horror, and anguish. He sees the tears that we keep hidden behind a mask.

How it thrills my heart to know that Jesus will one day be rewarded for all that He endured for us. One glorious day, we will see Him face to face and look into His beautiful eyes of love and tenderness. So, cheer up and be assured that it will be worth it all when we see Jesus! Have a good night's rest.

Let Your Life Be Your Living Testimony of God's Greatness

And the Lord thy God will make thee plenteous in every work of thine hand, in the fruit of thy body, and in the fruit of thy cattle, and in the fruit of thy land, for good: for the Lord will again rejoice over thee for good, as he rejoiced over thy fathers: If thou shalt hearken unto the voice of the Lord thy God, to keep his commandments and his statutes which are written in this book of the law, and if thou turn unto the Lord thy God with all thine heart, and with all thy soul. (Deuteronomy 30:9–10)

What is the secret to being happy? Is there a blueprint or winning formula for happiness? One fact is true: life can be unpredictable, so forgiveness is a key factor to living a great life. The inability to forgive or the unwillingness to forget what happened on the road of disappointment can lead to sleepless nights. Everyone knows at least one person who has convinced them that they cannot forgive or let go of their hurt feelings. (Often, the person one might need to forgive most is oneself!) A lot of people often say, "I can forgive you but can't forget what you've done!" That's not forgiving.

If you want your life to change for the better, it is imperative that you let go of whatever is slowing you down. Never let anyone convince you that holding on to negative events is a right that you should exercise. When you hold on to grudges, it is impossible to connect with people on a deeper level, which can result in shutting out the very people who care the most about you. You must remember also that forgiveness hinders your prayers. The Word of God says that when you stand praying, you must forgive.

Sometimes we can be so mad at the world that we refuse to allow the Holy Spirit to use us for the glory of God. Anger towards family members, friends, and colleagues could cause us to miss out on some of the greatest blessings coming our way.

When we embrace what God is doing in our lives all through the trials and tribulations, it will bring a smile to our faces. It is at that moment we realize that God is setting us up for something greater than we could ever imagine.

Let go and let God. Have a blessed night!

Now Is the Time

O Lord, thou hast searched me, and known me. Thou knowest my downsitting and mine uprising, thou understandest my thought afar off. Thou compassest my path and my lying down, and art acquainted with all my ways. For there is not a word in my tongue, but, lo, O Lord, thou knowest it altogether. Thou hast beset me behind and before, and laid thine hand upon me. (Psalm 139:1–5)

*R*ight where you are sitting or lying, declare with me, "No more distractions!" Now, commit to yourself that you will not allow negative people, negative situations, or negative events to distract you in this season. Distractions, whether big or small, are annoying and a waste of time. Lingering distractions plant negative seeds. They have the potential to weigh you down and stop you from moving forward in life. The Enemy is very clever in planting distractions all around you. Whether at home or work, distractions always seem to show up at the wrong time.

Distractions come to stress you and break your focus. The Enemy knows that from time to time you have allowed yourself to become stressed when things were not going your way. His overall goal is to get you to believe that things are worse than they appear.

I want to remind you that timing is everything. Let me rephrase that. Prophetic timing is everything. God has you on His mind in this season. What looked like a lost opportunity in the eyes of humankind was God's prophetic timing unfolding. The voice that you hear telling you to step out and take the risk is not the Enemy's. It is God's.

Before the foundation of the world, the Father's prophetic voice was released in your life, which cleared the way for you to have victory with every step you take. Allow me to give you some life-changing advice: in the realm of prophetic timing, do whatever God asks you to do!

The blessings that you are about to walk into could only have been designed in accordance with the prophetic timing of God. Years of frustration are being eliminated as you embark on your new journey. The way has been cleared. All you have to do is have the faith to continue to trust and follow God. Trust and do not doubt! Have a restful night!

Standing Up for What Is Right

*T*here's a popular song that says, "After you've done all you can, you just stand!"

In the world that we are living in today, it is especially hard when you stand up for what is right. People do wrong and expect to get right. You do what is right and you end up getting wrong. Twisted, isn't it? But in spite of any persecution, slander, verbal abuse, assassination of your character, false accusations, or lambasting, your heart and mind will be at ease knowing that you've done what is right and, more importantly, pleasing in the sight of God!

This life for many is a hard one. People get tired of being abused by the ones from whom they least expect abuse when they know within their hearts they've done nothing wrong.

The saints in the Bible were persecuted. They were killed and thrown in prison for doing right, but it did not deter them. They continued to stand up for the Word of God! As long as you know your heart is right with God, it doesn't matter if you are labelled otherwise.

You see, the anointing that is on your life cannot be removed by any words from human beings or by others' perceptions. After you've paid a price for your anointing, after you've fasted, prayed, and sought

God's face for it, you can't allow what other people say to cause you to feel that you are not called and chosen by God.

During times of persecution, remember that who God keeps is well kept. And don't be discouraged by what the Enemy says about you. Remember what God says about you, and endeavour to stand up for what is right!

After you've done all you can, just stand! Remember, the best pillow is a clear conscience!

God's Faithfulness

As I reflect tonight, all I can think about is the faithfulness of God. There are times in life when you are abandoned, left alone to bear your own burdens, to see and navigate your own way through life's storms, and to dodge life's hardballs. During times of abandonment, all you can do is let the tears flow as a sense of loneliness and oppression, and thoughts of giving up, floods your mind.

Ever felt low before, with shock and loss conspiring to carry off your hope that things will get better? Maybe you can relate. You may be saying, *I've been depressed like that before. I know the taste of ashes and the feeling of emptiness, and I remember wondering if God was with me.*

During these trying times, we all need to remember one person who will never abandon us—and that person is God! No matter what we've done or said, we can rest assured that He will never leave us or forsake us, especially during the times when we need Him most. Because He is faithful, He keeps up His side of the relationship even when we don't keep up ours. If we are faithless, He remains faithful— for He cannot deny Himself. Because He is faithful, we can depend on Him, count on Him, and look to Him to come through for us in every circumstance.

There are times when it feels as if the pain I feel inside will never leave me. In the moments when I just cry myself to sleep and then awake in the middle of the night, I get a sense of comfort knowing that God is faithful and He cannot go back on His Word, which says, "I will never leave you nor forsake you."

Let us rest tonight with the assurance that though people abandon us and let us down, God will never let us down!

What Are You Allowing to Rock Your Boat

*T*his journey we are on called life on earth is a complicated affair. Problems arise and issues occur in our lives that often place extreme pressure on us. And as human beings, we often complicate things by reasoning, analysing, and explaining everything.

Let us liken our life's problems to a storm. We, like the disciples, become fearful when the storms of life howl and the waves threaten us. We feel we are in control, thinking we can save ourselves. We think we can fix the problem on our own; we think we have all the answers; we think it's all up to us. Then we tend to put our hands on the rudder in case God doesn't know where He is going, just in case He takes too long. As a result, we complicate things.

I am stopping by tonight to remind you that in the storms of life, amidst the chaos of suffering, through all the temptations that you face in the unexpected hurricanes and the tornadoes of life that swirl against you, God is with you. You may think He is asleep and He is going to leave you to drown and die in your state, that He will leave you to bail the water out of the boat yourself. I want to encourage you tonight to become faithful and not fearful, because God with you.

What are you allowing to rock your boat? There are four things that we sometimes allow to rock our boats: fear, problems, sickness, and discouragement. Instead of allowing situations to rock your boat, you need to have faith in God.

We know who Jesus is. We know that He loves us. We know how He has helped us in the past. We have read His Word, and yet at times our faith is not quite strong enough and we, like the disciples, ask, "Teacher, don't You care if we drown?"

He cared enough to leave heaven for thirty-three hard years and spend that time as a man on earth. The One who created the universe and humankind knows what it is to walk in a human body and feel a human's desires, hungers, and fears. He shows us that no matter how dark and deep the trial, faith in and obedience to God can save every soul. Jesus was very much acquainted with our sorrows and pains. God lived as a man.

He cared enough to die for us. "Greater love has no one than this, that he lay down his life for his friends."(John 15:13). Whilst we were very much ungodly, Christ died for us. If He loved us enough to suffer, bear our sins, die, and then rise again, then how can we even think for a moment that He has forgotten us or that He no longer cares? Do you ask if Jesus cares? Does He really care?

When your heart is breaking, when the storms of life come crashing in, when your body is wracked with pain, when you feel that no one loves you, when your children are breaking your heart by walking contrary to their biblical upbringing, when you are about to lose your mind, when the doctors have given up on you, when you don't know where the next meal is coming from to feed your family, when all hell is breaking loose in your life, when folks turn their backs on you, when you are about to lose your home or your job, when you are at the point of taking your own life, when Satan keeps the same temptation boiling in your life, what do you do? Where do you turn?

The miracle of the calm sea did a lot for the apostles' faith. The storms in our lives are used by God to strengthen our faith. We either grow bitter or grow better. The choice is ours. We can panic or we can pray. We can bail water or we can bail out.

Let us be reminded that our loving Father knows our frame. He made us and knows just what we can take and endure. Have a restful night!

That Blessed Hope

*T*he world in which we are living in today is not a place that lends itself to hope. In fact, when you consider the death, diseases, natural disasters, and evil, and all the other negative things that fill our world, you see that there is just not a lot of room for hope.

So many go to bed at night with the hope that the next day will be better. We hope that our circumstances will change. We hope our bodies will get healed. We hope to see all that is wrong in our lives made right! Hope, hope, hope!

The dictionary defines *hope* as follows: "to have a wish to get or do something or for something to happen or be true, especially something that seems possible or likely"." Hope, from the world's viewpoint, is just what this definition describes. The world sees hope as a wish or a desire. Hope, as the world sees it, is a longing for something that may or may not take place.

In the face of the hopelessness that grips our world, there is one group of people who possess genuine hope: believers!

Even though we do not know what tomorrow will bring our way, we can still have hope once we put our faith and trust in God. It may bring death, disease, and disaster; it may bring sorrow, pain, and hardship; it may bring blessing, joy, and happiness. We may not know what tomorrow will bring, but we do know for sure that tomorrow will bring us that blessed hope found in Titus 2:13: "Looking for that blessed hope, and the glorious appearing of the great God and our Saviour Jesus Christ." When we prepare ourselves for the Lord's coming, all the stuff that we are faced with cannot compare with the joy we will experience in His glorious presence.

No matter what the circumstance may be, hope in God. He alone can satisfy your soul. He alone can heal your brokenness. He alone can heal your heart of all the hurt, anger, disappointment, and pain. Rest assured that Jesus loves you and He knows everything that you are faced with in your life! Hope thou in God! He truly loves you and care for you. People will fail you, but God will never fail you!

We Serve a Good God

Give, and it shall be given unto you; good measure, pressed down, and shaken together, and running over, shall men give into your bosom. For with the same measure that ye mete withal it shall be measured to you again. (Luke 6:38)

As I reflect tonight, my mind goes to how faithful God is to His Word, yet we as humans fail to consider that we must do our part in order for it to be fulfilled in our lives.

My mind goes to the scripture that reads, "Give and it shall be given." That is a promise I have seen be fulfilled in my life over and over again. Yet some people think they don't have to do their part—but they must.

We must be mindful of the fact that every command God gives us in His Word is for our good. He is a good God, and He works all things together for our good because He loves us. He wants to bless us, multiply us, and fill us with His exceeding joy and peace, but we have to do our part. We have to obey His commands in order to set the blessing into motion.

When the world is going through financial crisis, we Christians don't have to worry because we've made our deposits in the bank of heaven and are awaiting the return. (hallelujah!). I know a lot of people pull back when they hear us as pastors preach about or mention money from the pulpit, but money is a part of God's way of blessing us.

When I reflect on that scripture, I see it also goes beyond money. I think of it as talking about anything we give. We have to sow good seeds in our daily walk with God and the blessings will come to us.

One of the best ways to see the blessing of God operating in your life is by sowing a seed of your time, abilities, or resources. Proverbs says that those who scatter seed generously reap even more. That's because when you give, God promises that it will come back to you in abundance—pressed down, shaken together, and running over. But you have to freely receive in order to have something to give. It works both ways.

The more we freely receive from God, the more we desire to freely give to others.

Tonight as you go to sleep, I encourage you to keep your heart and mind open to what God has for you. Look for ways to sow seeds. Freely give and set the blessing in motion in your life today!

Forgiveness

And forgive us our debts, as we forgive our debtors.
(Matthew 6:12)

*I*n life, unfair things happen to us all. We can choose to hold on to the hurt, become bitter and angry, and let it poison our future, or we can choose to let it go and trust God to make it up to us. Perhaps you think that you are able to forgive because someone hurt you so badly.

I have had the most terrible things done and said to me throughout my lifetime, and I had to forgive the people who did and said those things. If I hadn't forgiven, then my prayers would have been hindered. We must forgive if we want our heavenly Father to forgive us.

Many people tend to say, "I will forgive you, but I cannot forget what you've done." Well, as human beings it is hard to forget what someone said or did to us, whether good or bad, but in the end we should not allow what they said or did to consume us and cause us not to forgive them.

There may be some who will never ask for your forgiveness, but in your heart you have to forgive them—if not for their sake, then for yours.

I want to share an experience I had where I was hurt by an individual who never asked me for forgiveness. Even though the person never asked me for forgiveness, I forgave him. Unfortunately, that individual died. I wept when I heard of his demise. Why? Because the memory of the hurt flooded my mind, and more importantly the memory of what the hurt caused me flooded my mind. Believe it or not, that person appeared in one of my dreams. He just stood there. I asked him, "What was the matter?" He did not reply, just walked away. The next night he appeared in my dreams again, and whilst I was dreaming, the Holy Spirit told me what the person wanted. I told him I had forgiven him years ago and that he could rest in peace. I haven't seen this person in any of my dreams since. I call that the power of forgiveness.

I've experienced other unpleasant moments in my life which affected me mentally, but I had to let them go so that I could move on in the path which has been ordained for my life.

You might say, "You don't know how I was raised," or "My ex-spouse caused me a lot of pain," or "This friend betrayed me," or "I just can't let it go." But realize, you don't forgive for the other person's sake; you forgive for your own sake. When you forgive, you are taking away the other person's power to hurt you. But if you hold on to that offence and stay angry, you are only poisoning your own life and disconnecting yourself from God.

Forgiveness is like a door in your heart. If you shut the door and refuse to forgive, then God cannot forgive you. But when you open the door and allow forgiveness to flow from you, then His forgiveness can flow into you. Choose to forgive and open the door to receiving God's life, peace, and healing today. No one and nothing is worth your not being able to get forgiveness, answers to your prayers, or peace of mind.

So as you go to sleep tonight, let go of all the hurt and pain you have experienced from others, and thank God for the gift of forgiveness that sets you free. Ask Him to help you to truly understand what it means to forgive so you can receive forgiveness. Have a restful night.

What Are You Filling Your Life With?

*T*his is a question I ask myself often: "What am I filling my life with?" God always wants to bless us and multiply us. He wants to increase us above and beyond what we could ever ask, think, or imagine. But sometimes, we fill our lives with so much that we simply don't have room to receive all that God wants to give us.

People fill their lives with good things, noteworthy obligations, and impressive accomplishments. But "good" can be the enemy of "best". We have to take the time to evaluate what we have in our hands and be willing to drop some of those things in order to make room for the new thing God has for us. I love the scripture that says, "God wants to do a new thing." I went further with it one time when I used this scripture as a text for a sermon, by asking, "Who will let Him?"

We are living in a season when we all are to allow God's will and purpose to fill our lives. Living from day to day without purpose, without reason, and also without positively affecting the world we're living in will be in vain.

Tonight, take some time to evaluate your life before going to sleep. Be open to what God wants to do in you and through you. If your hands are full, maybe it's time to use what you have to bless other people.

Don't let holding on to yesterday keep you from God's best. Instead, make room, because He has abundant blessings in store for you.

As you seek God in prayer tonight, open your hands and your heart to Him. Choose to release anything spiritual, physical, or emotional that would keep you from your best. Ask Him to search your heart and show you where you need to make adjustments to make room for Him.

Have a peaceful night.

Are Your Steps Ordered by the Lord?

We live our lives sometimes as if we are the ones who are in control of our beings, of what we do and say, and of where we go.

I want to remind you tonight that as a child of the Most High God, your steps are ordered by Him. He has a specific place of blessing prepared for you. When you live a life of obedience to the Word of God, He promises to supply every one of your needs. Just as God directed Elijah to his place of blessing, God is directing you, too.

You may be lying there asking yourself with tears flowing down your cheeks, "How am I going to feed my family for the next few days?" or "How am I going to pay my bills?" I want you to know that God knows everything that you are in need of.

Be assured that He's aligning the right opportunities for you and causing the right people to come along your path to help you get ahead. He's constantly working behind the scenes on your behalf. But you have to do your part to keep your heart open by following His Word and keeping an attitude of faith and expectancy. A major key to keeping your heart in the right place is choosing peace and unity. The Bible says that when you live in unity with others, it is there that He has commanded the blessing. And when your heart is in the place of blessing, the rest of your life will be in the place of blessing too. Today, choose peace, choose obedience, and choose the place of blessing.

You don't have to be burdened down with the cares of life. If God takes care of the lilies of the field and the sparrows, be assured that He cares about you and your needs.

The scripture reminds us that our God shall supply all your needs according to His riches in glory by Christ Jesus.

I remember one time in my low days when I did not have a dollar to feed myself or my daughter. It was so bad that icing sugar was what I had to use to sweeten our drinks. The freezer was empty and there was no food in the cupboards, and believe it or not, I had no one to turn to ask for help.

I prayed and reminded God of His Word, and I can testify to you and say that before I left my house for work, a Christian woman with a big box in her hand knocked on my door. Everything that I needed to eat and take care of my girl with was in that box. All I could do was praise God as tears of joy came down my face. He proved to me once again that He had me on His mind. I asked the woman how she knew. She said, "Whilst in prayer, the Holy Spirit spoke to me." That's the kind of God we serve. Just trust Him.

As you go to bed tonight, lay your cares at His feet in faith, and He will come through for you. Have a restful night.

I Will Give You Life

So many people today are looking for ways to prolong their lives and renew their youth, but God already has a fail-proof system outlined in His Word. It says in Isaiah that when we put our hope in Him, He will renew our youth.

"My son, forget not my law; but let thine heart keep my commandments: For length of days, and long life, and peace, shall they add to thee" (Proverbs 3:1–2).

This verse doesn't say that you will just have a long, drawn-out, ordinary life. No, God promises that He will prolong your life and fill your days with peace and prosperity. He wants you to live a fulfilled life and be happy all the days of your life. That's why it's so important to keep His Word first place in your life. You mustn't allow distractions to steal your focus or get you off course.

Tonight before falling to sleep, choose to keep His commands in your heart, and enjoy His peace and prosperity all the days of your life.

Thank Him for giving you a long, satisfying life. Choose to honour Him and to keep His Word first place in your life. Ask Him to show you His ways so that you may walk with Him all the days of your life. Have a restful life.

Purpose in Your Pain

*I*just want to remind you tonight before going to sleep that I know that there are times when you wonder when the trials will end. You ask, "When will I experience 'heaven on earth'? When will happiness come through my door? When? When? When?" If you are wondering, remember that God is never late: He's always on time! Delay is not denial! Hold on for a little while longer. God has not forgotten you! There is purpose in the pain!

There are times when life hits us with one trial after the other. We sometimes ask God why. There are times when it seems as if the trials will never stop, as if the pain and agony we feel inside will never go away.

I've had many nights like that, nights when I thought I wouldn't wake up the next morning, nights when I felt as if the world around me was crashing in on me because of the number of false perceptions that had been formed against me, the ridicule of society, and my having been abandoned by those who said they were my friends.

I had to forge my way through those dark times. I had to rely totally on God, even though I couldn't feel Him and couldn't hear Him. I felt that He had left me. Then one day He assured me that He had been with me, carrying me through that difficult, painful period in my life.

As I look back now, I see there was purpose in the pain I endured. There was purpose in all that I went through for a year and half.

I can now help others who are going through the circumstances I experienced and other circumstances related to those. I can assure each person who is going through such circumstances, or who may one day go through them, that one has to experience that pain in order to be an encourager or counsellor to someone else.

You cannot testify or relate to anything if you've never experienced it. Therefore, instead of asking God, "Why me?" say to Him, "Why not me?" There is purpose in whatever it is you're going through. You can ask God to carry you through it and just have faith to believe that He is doing so.

Rest well tonight, knowing that God has got you and that everything will be OK in the end.

Have a blessed night!

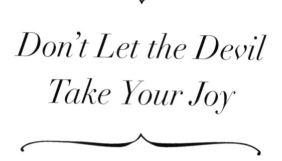

Don't Let the Devil Take Your Joy

The Lord is my strength and my shield; my heart trusted in him, and I am helped: therefore my heart greatly rejoiceth; and with my song will I praise him. (Psalm 28:7)

*L*ife presents you with many ups and downs. It is how you handle the ups and downs that makes the difference in your life. It does not matter where you are presently, you can still make right choices that will benefit your life. Never let the downs get you so depressed that you stop yourself from excelling. Start seeing your life as a skyscraper that is being built from the ground up.

It takes a lot of imagination and innovation to build a skyscraper. That which you can imagine being done can be done. Your life has been designed to stand tall and handle the storms of life. Your structure has been built on a solid foundation of prayer, faith, and mental toughness.

The Bible reminds us, "Wisdom is the principal thing; therefore, get wisdom. And in all your getting, get understanding" (Proverbs 4:7). Never allow yourself to go into a deep depression simply because you think the grass is greener in your neighbour's yard. You must not judge your success based on another person's résumé. You have heard stories about how others have tried to do it but failed to get that job, for example. They were talked out of it. I hear the Spirit saying, "That will not be your story."

Remember, you are the architect of your own success. The Enemy will do his best to rob you of your joy and excitement. So much has been loaded on your plate that it might seem overwhelming, but remember that the steps of a righteous person are ordered by the Lord.

The Enemy knows that if he can stop you or slow you down with unpredictable happenstances, there is a chance that you will begin to see your life as failing. You would think that by now he would have left you alone. Surely, he can see that your joy cannot be taken away from you. Do not let the Enemy take your joy. Your happiness rests in your relationship with the Father.

Many have tried, and many will try again. Stay the course, because God has your back! Don't fall for the trick of selling your birthright. It is not worth it. Your greater days are ahead of you. Have a blessed night!

Your Aroma

*M*y mind is weighing heavy tonight as I am thinking on the woman who broke her alabaster box and anointed Jesus and how she was despised for having done so. She used this costly ointment which she had saved up for years and waited until such time to anoint the Saviour in the days leading up to His death and burial.

There's a line in a song that goes, "You don't know the cost of the oil in my alabaster box." Many people have suffered throughout their lives, and despite what they were faced with, they endured it and made it through. Right now you may be thinking about me, *You are always talking about suffering.* Suffering is a process that God uses to get us where He wants us to be.

The anointing that is upon a person's life doesn't come with the snap of a finger; it is borne through sweat and tears. We should never look at another's person life and be jealous of how God may be using him or her, because we don't know what that person has endured to reach that level in God!

What really stands out to me is the aroma that emanated from the box when the woman broke it. It filled the entire place with a sweet scent. As I think about this, the question comes to my mind "What type of aroma is smelt when you break your alabaster box? Does your presence make those around want to sniff, or does it cause them to cover their noses because it is unpleasant?" Tough question!

It is very sad when we are in the presence of people who are supposed to radiate love and emit an aroma that should cause us to want to sniff, but instead we seek to cover our noses. That's a serious thing. I personally know what it is to be looked at and treated as if I don't exist, but it is my desire to be a person who brings a sweet aroma to anyone who is around me.

Despite what you may go through in this life, don't allow the ills to change who you are. Don't allow the attitudes of others and the way they treat you to change you from the sweet, loving person you are! Let your aroma leave those around you sniffing and wanting more! Make a difference no matter what. Have a sweet restful sleep tonight, and be blessed!

Jesus, Take the Wheel

*T*here comes a time in your life when you get very tired of the same thing happening over and over and over again. No matter what good you do, no matter how kind and generous you are in this life you face disappointments, are accused falsely, are taken for granted, are looked down on, are hurt, are thrown under the bus, etc. In times like these, you wonder, *Why is this happening to me? What have I done to make this life so unhappy, unfair, unkind, and burdensome?*

I am reminded of a song that is usually sung at funerals: "Farther along we'll know all about it. Farther along we'll understand why." But we get so tired of things happening to us over and over again. It seems as if there is no end to turmoil.

In times like these, we really need Jesus to take the wheel, because if the wheel were to remain in our hands, we just might end up crashing. We are headed for disaster or even are on the road to dying. The comfort in such times in our lives comes from knowing that God knows our hearts. We do nothing, we fear nothing! You see, humankind looks on the outward appearance, but God looks at the heart. This fact helps to keep us sane and helps to keep us from not giving up on God. Because if we allow the difficult situation to do so, it will have a negative effect on us.

There is a song that says, "It's a hard world we're living in. People get hurt again and again." Make up your mind whether you're going to be weak or strong.

Sometimes you think you're weak, but the truth of the matter is that if you are still in your right mind and you're still standing, you're strong after all you have had to face in life.

It is good to lay your head on your pillow at night with a freed mind. The best pillow is a clear conscience. One of the things you have to remember is what the Bible says: "Forgive, forgive." Let go and let God take the wheel.

Unforgiveness

*I*f we allow bitterness towards a person or situation to remain in our hearts, it can overtake the joyful parts of our lives.

Hanging onto bitterness doesn't improve the situation—it doesn't bring justice or exact revenge. We need to be able to catch bitterness early on so we can uproot it before it hurts us and others. This is where forgiveness comes in. Forgiving others doesn't mean that what they did to us was OK, but it does set us free from bitterness, which if allowed to fester will only hurt us more. The people who suffer most from unforgiveness are us.

Why should we forgive?

"For if ye forgive men their trespasses, your heavenly Father will also forgive you: But if ye forgive not men their trespasses, neither will your Father forgive your trespasses" (Matthew 6:14–15).

We forgive because Jesus chose to forgive us when we didn't deserve it. If we want to reflect the life of Jesus every day, we should be willing to forgive others when they don't deserve it.

How do we forgive others?

Forgiveness does not always happen instantaneously—it's a process and a daily choice. True forgiveness happens when we partner with God by asking Him to help us forgive others as He has forgiven us.

It all comes down to an act of repetition. Because we're human and it's easy to fall back into bitterness, we'll have to come back to God regularly and ask for His help with forgiving.

Unfortunately, we probably won't feel forgiveness the first time we say we forgive someone—but that's because forgiveness is a partnership with God. If we commit to thinking it and saying it, God will honour our commitment and help us truly forgive.

Forgiveness is not a lack of boundaries. You can forgive someone and not pursue a friendship with the person, go out with him or her again, work for him or her again, etc.

Forgiveness is not weakness. Actually, forgiving others means you're strong! Because you are willing to let go of the past and your hurt, you're choosing to focus your heart on greater things.

Forgiveness is not easy, but it's a necessary part of healing a broken heart. Ask God to help you work towards forgiveness.

Be Empowered

We serve a God of abundance! He is more than enough! No matter what is on your plate in life, God wants to pour out His abundant grace upon you. One of the meanings of grace is God's goodwill, loving-kindness, and favour.

I often say that too many people take God's grace for granted. When I say that, I mean that because people know that His grace is extended to them daily, they think they can live any kind of life, being in and out of His will, doing their own thing, and life for them will still be grand. And when they've had enough of the world, they can step back into His way for their lives.

I want remind you tonight that His grace keeps you, strengthens you, and causes you to increase. In fact, He's already extending that grace to you right now. All you have to do is open your heart and humbly receive it by faith and remain faithful.

Being humble is an important key to receiving God's grace. If we are seeking our own way, it blocks Him from working in our lives. But when we are humble, then He will empower us by His grace. His Word tells us that by His grace we will have everything that we need at all times. That's living in abundance! And when we are living in abundance, we are equipped to be a blessing to those around us.

Tonight before you go to sleep, seek His ways first and allow Him to empower you by His grace. He is right there, willing and able to do that for you.

Have a restful night!

Serving God

There's a part of an old hymn that says, "The longer I serve Him, the sweeter He grows. The longer I love Him, the more love He bestows. Each day is like heaven. My heart overflows. The longer I serve Him, the sweeter He grows."

This Christian walk that we are on is not an easy one. There are many who started out on this journey but then turned back when the road got rough and tough to travel. My thoughts tonight are in reference to my own life. There were times I failed. There were times when I fell but I got back up again. Sometimes when I think about my life, I say to myself, *If I didn't have Jesus Christ in my life, I would be messed up, out of my mind, and probably sleeping in my grave!*

I got saved as a child at the age of nine. Yes, that's young. I grew up in church. I know no other life than to serve God. As I said before, there were times when I fell, but I got back up because Jesus had His hand on my life and He wouldn't let me go. I am not saying that my life is perfect and everything is perfect, but one thing I know is that the longer I serve Christ, the sweeter He grows.

You may be weary on this road because of the pressures of life, but I want to encourage you not to give up on God. He is counting on you. He loves you. The easiest thing to do is to give up, but the best thing to do is to hold on to God. There is nothing that's going on in your life that He can't handle. It will be worth it all when you see His face one day and live with Him in heaven.

Perhaps you don't know Christ. Now is the expected time to find Him. Receive Him now. I can guarantee you that it will be the best thing ever to happen to you. He is a Friend who will never leave you or forsake you. He will be your burden-bearer, your mind regulator, your lawyer, your doctor, your true lover, and your Father.

I have never regretted serving God, and I am thankful that I've accepted Him as my personal Lord and Saviour. Try Jesus!

Desire to Change

*M*ost people have things in their lives that they want to change—old habits, addictions, or something else they want to overcome. These are situations that people are faced with regularly. The world offers so many "solutions" to improve a person's life, but really, the only way a person is truly changed, the only way to be permanently transformed, is to renew one's mind with the Word of God.

In the Bible, there is a solution for every trial you may be faced with in your life. There was a period in my life when I had to fall asleep with the audio Bible playing in order for my mind to get renewed to face the next day. As I reflect on that period in my life, my heart is overwhelmed because I know what so many are going through.

The scripture tells us that we shouldn't follow the pattern of the world. What is the pattern of the world? It's the constant striving to do more, be more, and have more that leads only to weariness, emptiness, and frustration. That's not what God intends! Instead, focus your thoughts on the Word of God, because when you make the Word your number one focus, something supernatural takes place.

Only you can control the doorway to your mind. Nobody can do this for you. You choose what you meditate on and what you set before your eyes. I encourage you to stay on the offensive and diligently guard your mind and heart, because when you do things God's way, you get God's results—life, peace, and joy!

I'm Glad I've Counted the Cost

The song "I'm Glad I've Counted the Cost" is a song many Christians love to sing. But when I meditate on the lyrics, it causes me to really think about the part that says, "I've paid the price and obtained the prize. He saved my soul that was lost, and now my treasures are in the sky. I'm glad I've counted the cost."

Have we really counted the costs? Whilst we are living here below, there is still a cost to pay. As we think about our brothers and sisters in Christ who are being beheaded for Christ, if such a prospect reaches us, will we pay the price?

I sometimes think about my life and stuff I have endured and continue to endure, and sometimes say it's unfair, hard, and unbearable. Sometimes I ask myself, *Why do I have to go through something like this? It seems that it will never end.*

There is a reason for everything we go through in life. It is either to perfect us or to prepare us to help someone else. It is there so that something greater may come to us and prepare us for ministry. Someone said that if you are a true soldier, you will go through difficult times. I am a solider in the army of the Lord. If you are too, then you will go through tough times. You will count the cost.

Like Job, let us be determined that when He tries us, we will come forth as pure gold. The Word of God declares, "Behold, I have refined thee, but not with silver; I have chosen thee in the furnace of affliction" (Isaiah 48:10).

You are being afflicted now, but it will not be so forever. However long your trials may seem to last, they will surely come to an end—a profitable end.

The furnace of affliction will not ruin us but will refine our faith. I truly believe God wants to burn away any distractions or doubts we may have. As all these impurities burn away, the image of God's Son will be more clearly revealed in us.

Though we may find ourselves on the anvil of suffering, we should know that God has not abandoned us. He is not being cruel to us. He is at work. He knows just how hot the fire should be and how long we must be in it. He is extracting all the impurities from us to fit us for an eternity in His presence in heaven.

> I cast on Jesus my every care.
> I'm glad I counted the cost.
> And all my burdens He helps to bear.
> I'm glad I counted the cost.
>
> 'Twill not be long till the Lord shall come.
> I'm glad I counted the cost.
> And bear my soul to that heav'nly home.
> I'm glad I counted the cost.

I pray that we will allow God our Refiner to plunge us into the fires of difficulty if He must. I pray that He will forgive us in advance for our moments of doubting His process. I am trusting that the fires will not leave us deformed but will cause us to be transformed into the image of God's Son.

Hiding in God's Presence

Thou art my hiding place; thou shalt preserve me from trouble; thou shalt compass me about with songs of deliverance. (Psalm 32:7)

He that dwelleth in the secret place of the most High shall abide under the shadow of the Almighty. (Psalm 91:1)

One of the most precious gifts Jesus gave to us when He ascended into heaven was His presence in the person of the Holy Spirit. Yet there are many of us who forget that when we see trouble on every side and are beset with the cares of this life, there is an escape for us in the presence of the Lord. We so often forget that there is a place in God for us to take shelter in. I want to remind you that in the Lord's presence there is fullness of joy, a joy that supersedes all your worries, fears, disappointments, heartbreaks, sicknesses, oppression, and depression. His presence makes us whole.

Life is filled with challenges and dangers, with failures and tragedies. We who live this life in relationship with God are not immune to suffering, but God is our hiding place. In Him we also find refuge and shelter from the world's influence, our sinful nature, and Satan our enemy.

As you lay your head down to rest tonight, let go of all the cares of this life and thank God for being your hiding place, your place of safety and security. For it is in God that we find rest, even in the midst of life's turmoil and troubles.

There's a hymn that says, "He will hide me, safely hide me, where the storms will never betide me, in the shelter of His arms." Have a sweet sleep in God's arms tonight!

Our Shepherd

So often we repeat the Twenty-Third Psalm as if it's a memory gem, but in it there is much truth and assurance for each of us. God loves us so much that He gave to us a Shepherd. Christ was appointed to be our Shepherd by God the Father, and by His saving grace He was submissive to the cross.

There is so much we can glean from this psalm and to apply to every area of our lives. We sometimes unnecessarily suffer because we fail to take God at His word.

Our Lord Jesus Christ is omniscient, and as God He knows all His sheep and their infirmities, their needs, and their weaknesses. When we are lost, He knows where to find us. When we are in need, He knows what to supply. When we are hungry, He knows what to feed us. His love for us is pure, and as God, He is omnipotent and has all power in heaven and on earth. He saves us from all harm; He protects us from all evil; He defends us and rescues us. He is our all in all. All knowledge and wisdom is His. He will guide us and direct us for His name's sake. He is the Great Shepherd, the Chief Shepherd, and the Good Shepherd—and we are the sheep of His pasture.

As we lie before the Lord tonight and sleep closes in on us, let us repeat this psalm with confidence that the Lord is truly our Shepherd. Have a restful night!

Bridging the Gap

But seek ye first the kingdom of God, and his righteousness; and all these things shall be added unto you. (Matthew 6:33)

So many times when we think our life is in a mess, we see many people who wish their lives were half as good as ours. If today we were to do an anonymous poll on who's happy and who's not, I believe the result of that poll would be alarming as to how many folks are living a lie.

We are all in pursuit of happiness. In some way or form, we are constantly moving towards what we believe will make us happy, either in the short term or in the long term. You might say that we are designed for happiness and that since the beginning of time human beings have devised countless ways and means of creating happiness. For the majority of us, happiness comes in the form of what we call success, by achieving certain things that we believe will make us happy.

When you are fulfilled, your life is one of the deepest joy because you feel as if it is fully worth living and that you are fulfilling a greater purpose. You feel that you are realizing the reason why you came here. A question so many ask is "Why am I here?"

On a deep level we all know what we love and what we hate. Yet, so many people are stuck in careers that they hate or stay in relationships with people they will never be in harmony with. In this regard, people know that they hate it, but still they do it—and often they have "good reasons" for this.

The truth is that as long as you are in this category, you will never be happy, because you know that what you are doing is something you hate.

But the way to live a happy and fulfilled life, my friend, can only be found in Jesus Christ. He alone can give you life more abundantly. The Word says when you seek God's kingdom first and all His righteousness, all things will be added unto you. That means everything that will cause you to be happy, and the fulfilment that you so desire, is in Christ, who is the answer.

Have a blessed night!

Grace in a Barren Place

For this entry, first read 2 Samuel 9:1–9, 13:2. The text focuses on two main characters, David and Mephibosheth, the grandson of Saul and son of Jonathan respectively, and on a place called Lodebar.

Mephibosheth is a picture of us, the fallen human race; David is a picture of King Jesus; and Lodebar is a picture of the state of the church today in the end times, which is the church many of the saints are part of.

It is a story about the distress that is experienced because of change. It is a story about an invitation that was accepted. It is a story about friendship, promises, grace, love, compassion, forgiveness, and hope.

So seldom in the profile about David do we see such kindness. David is generally thought of as the little shepherd who slew the giant, or as the man who committed adultery with Bathsheba or ran from Saul. We remember him as being a man after God's own heart, relocating the Ark of the Covenant to Jerusalem, having many wives, seeing incest in his family between his sons and daughters, and having a friendship with Jonathan the son of Saul. It is this friendship with Jonathan that brings us to this account tonight.

In earlier chapters of the book of 2 Samuel, we see a very beautiful friendship between Jonathan and David. We know that they were close because the scripture gives us an account of how they loved each other as the two were of one soul. David and Jonathan had bonded together and were very loyal to one another in spite of how Saul felt about David. David and Jonathan had made a covenant of friendship to each other, promising that the one who survived or outlived the other would look after the other's family.

This incident certainly stands as a challenge to us as to how we operate with our friends and what kinds of promises we have made and kept and/or broken. It is also a challenge to honour the promises that we made to our own parents, grandparents, and descendants, showing that to do so reflects how we also keep our promises to God.

We are certainly living in a time where all relationships are suspect and challenged. If you have a friend, it just seems as if everyone is wondering what is going on between the two of you as if there is no such thing as pure friendship. (Am I telling the truth?) It is equally a concern when friends are friends regardless of the problems and perceptions of others. You know how it is, people want you to be mad at your friend because they are, and they do not seem to understand it when you say, "But that doesn't have anything to do with me." People want you to be mad at a whole family in our society today because they have problems with one member of the family. We just can't seem to separate the issues and deal with them.

At any rate, this story in the Bible is about a time of much turmoil. Saul had failed as the first king, and David is now king. Jonathan and Saul had died in the same battle on Mount Gilboa. Mephibosheth was only five years old at the time. It was chaotic: the king was dead, the prince was dead, and now the people were wondering, *What will happen to us?* The nurse picks up the child and, whilst everyone is running for their lives, drops Mephibosheth.

Although she saves his natural life, he is now crippled for life. Mephibosheth belonged to the royal line and thus lived in exile and in fear of King David. He was subject to persecution and slander but was rescued because of a promise that had been made to his father that he probably never even had heard about. Mephibosheth would still have been in trouble if David kept promises like we keep them today. We have trouble keeping our promises to each other to each other's face, but David was faced with the challenge of keeping his promise now that his friend is dead.

Most kings in the time of David tried to completely destroy the families of their rivals in order to prevent any of the descendants from trying to regain the throne. David did not do this; he actively sought out the descendants of his friend. He was told that Jonathan had a son but that the son was alive but lame.

His search landed his servants down in Lodebar, a city east of the Jordan River characterized by its barrenness, wasteland, and devastation. Lodebar was a city in the midst of the wilderness. It was a place of no pasture, no greenery. It was desolate in Lodebar. Down in Lodebar, Mephibosheth lost his rank, his prestige, his respectability, his reputation, his superiority, and his self-will. Down in Lodebar, Mephibosheth went from living in a palace to hiding out with a family friend; from a prince to a servant; and from powerful to afraid.

Now in Lodebar, the orphan Mephibosheth was found and afraid for his life. David did not want to take his life but wished to save it and by restoring to him all that had been taken from him. Just like God, who wants to restore to us all belonging to us that the cankerworm and palmer has eaten. Mephibosheth was going to have to trust David. Mephibosheth was summoned to the palace and was received because of David's deep love for Mephibosheth's father. Turn to your neighbour and tell them, "You never know where your blessing is coming from. That's why you'd better be kind to everybody."

When Mephibosheth, now twenty years old, whose name means "he scatters shame" or "destroyer of shame", came face to face with David, he fell flat on the floor in an act of submission. He referred to himself as a dead dog, meaning he felt that he had no worth or value. Dogs then were not held in such high regard as they are now. Dogs didn't have their own houses, clothes, doctors, and food, and didn't living in the owners' homes and the like. That was when a dog was a dog. Dogs were actually disliked and held in contempt. Mephibosheth was comparing himself to something very lowly and helpless.

He really didn't know how things were going to work out. All he knew was that kings had a way of destroying the remnants of their successors' families. But he humbled himself, fell on his face, reverenced the king, and confessed his unworthiness. David quickly put Mephibosheth at ease, offered forgiveness, and invited him to dine at the king's table and be cared for, for the rest of his natural life. He was accepted and adopted into the royal family. David took him to the throne and gave him back everything that had been taken.

My question to you is, have you been dropped severely in life to the point that it crippled you? Are you in a state of Lodebar, where there is a dryness in your Christian life? Are you in dry dock, so to speak? Saints of God, God is calling each and every one of us today to wholeness. He wants to take us from that desolate place and bring us to eat at His table.

Today, like Mephibosheth, you may have been dropped by a parent or friends, or maybe a family member—they have abandoned you; they have rejected you. You may feel as if society—the system of society—has dropped you. If you aren't the best, you are the rest. You have been dropped from the ladder of moving up.

You may feel as if you've been dropped by not having been given the opportunity to excel in your education. Perhaps none of your family, your relatives, care for you. You may even feel as if God has forsaken you—your prayers are not answered, your dreams and visions do not come true. It seems as if the Word of God fails you. You feel as if God has dropped you.

Your crippled state speaks of your woundedness, your brokenness, and your inability to carry on in life as normal. Today, are you in a crippled state? Has sin in your life crippled you so that you cannot come near to Jesus? Today, have you been dropped in any way, whether ruthlessly or accidentally, by people, by life? Do you feel you have been abandoned, forsaken, forgotten, wounded, and disappointed? If so, you are Mephibosheth—the crippled child.

This story of David and Mephibosheth does not end here. Mephibosheth is really a picture of you and me before God. Until we become who we are supposed to be in God, we are in exile in Lodebar. We are living against God's will for our lives and we are looked on as enemies. An enemy in this case includes any person who displeases God and breaks His commandments. Mephibosheth was one of the enemy, but David had a special invitation waiting for him. God also has an invitation for us to renew us, restore us, and refresh us. God needs our hands, our mouths, and every part of us to be used in these end times. We cannot work for Him whilst we are in Lodebar.

This story is placed here to show us a type of salvation that is available to us through Christ Jesus. Like David, we are searched for by our Lord until He finds us. Like David did, Jesus, once He finds us, tries to have a little talk with us.

Then if we are willing and ready, our Lord Jesus redeems us. Jesus restores us and returns us to our Father's table in peace. We also are heirs to our heavenly Father's kingdom. But somebody dropped us whilst we were running for our lives.

David's love was exemplary of the love of God. It came out of a merciful heart. He didn't have to find Jonathan's son. Nobody else was there when he made the covenant. Nobody but David knew what he had promised. Nobody would have even cared. After the way Saul had tried to kill David twenty-three times, David could have said, "Forget the whole thing. Let them make it the best way they can." But David was gracious and sought out the undeserving and gave all that could have been his. Only God can touch a person and make him do this kind of deed. Mephibosheth was lifted from poverty to plenty through the grace of the king.

Every day God shows us kindness and mercy. We are undeserving, but He keeps on blessing us anyway. We are undeserving, but He keeps on keeping us. We are undeserving, but He keeps on striving with us. We are undeserving, but He keeps on forgiving us. We are undeserving, but He keeps on loving us. He keeps on coming where we are to bless us and lift us up. God in His loving-kindness offers us everlasting life in His family and asks us to dine at His royal table for the rest of our lives. The choice is ours. We have fallen and are crippled, but we don't have to stay down and remain that way.

We are lame from our falls. We were running for our lives. We got so busy running that we tripped and fell. We have fallen into trouble. We have fallen into confusion. We have fallen outside the will of God. We have fallen into sin. We have fallen into yokes and burdens. We have fallen for our own ways instead of God's way. We have fallen into curses. We have fallen into pride.

You may have even been carried and dropped: dropped by someone who was trying to save you; dropped by someone else's fall; dropped by someone else's sins; dropped into a place where you didn't belong. Now you can't walk straight. You feel so down and out that your spiritual strength and hope is lost. Every time you try to get on your feet, you fall down. Every time you try to walk, you fall down. Every time you make a vow to the Lord, you find yourself having to take it back, Every time you promise the Lord "I won't do that anymore," you fall down. Every time you endeavour to do the right thing, wrong kicks you all over again and laughs in your face.

You may be content in Lodebar because you are alive, but I am admonishing you to get up. I know you are crippled by despair; I know you are crippled by sickness or disease; I know you are crippled by things from your past; I know you are crippled by desires that won't turn you loose; I know you are in pain. I implore you, I invite you, I entreat you, come on out of Lodebar.

You can come out! Come on, you can come on out. The Enemy may have you feeling feel like you are nothing. I know that you feel that you are nobody. I know that you've been walked on. I know that you have been down so long that you don't even know which way is up. But come on, come on, come on: you can come out of Lodebar today. You don't belong there. You belong in the King's palace of grace and mercy, and you can come back. Come out of Lodebar; there's nothing but death for you there. Come out of Lodebar; there's only defeat for you there. Come out of Lodebar, where there is wasteland. Come out of Lodebar; there is no pasture there. Come out. Even in the valley, there are green pastures in God. Come out of Lodebar and into a pure relationship with God. Come out of Lodebar and into victory over Satan. Come out of Lodebar and into victory in Jesus.

Satan wants you to think that you won't make it outside of Lodebar. But come on out. You can make it. God has something better for you. God has a way out for you. You don't have to die in that state.

God wants to use you. There is much work to do in the kingdom. The time is drawing nigh. Don't stay in the state that you're in. You are in the Potter's house, and the Potter wants to put you back together again. God has prepared a way of escape for you. Just walk in it. Just walk—crawl like Mephibosheth if you have to—but come out. God has a place for you in His palace.

If a storm is raging in your life, pray and read the Bible more. Stand strong in your faith in Christ. Look around for others who are suffering too and pray for them. Don't be discouraged when it seems there is no hope. God can make a way in the wilderness or through the darkness. When you are going through hard times, take your eyes off your circumstances and put them on the Lord and His Word. Believe His truth above whatever you are experiencing. This doesn't mean denying your circumstances; it means believing that God's Word triumphs over all. Rise above it. Jesus Christ is still Lord of all! Amen!

Pray and ask the Lord to help you to stand strong in all you know about yourself. Acknowledge that you are weak, and rejoice that He is strong in you—especially during times of trial and difficulty. Ask Him to help you to learn what you need to know from each challenge you face in your life. Ask Him to lift you out of any hopelessness, fear, doubt, or frustration. Ask Him to help you to stand strong so that you can stand without wavering, no matter what happens. Ask Him to fill you with courage and faith, and rejoice in the Lord.

Don't Allow Anyone to Vandalize Your Wonderful Heart

*I*n this life you will find a lot of people who live from day to day allowing their hearts to be trampled on. As an individual, there are moments in your life when you need to pause and do an inventory of yourself. You must not life each day, week, month, and year not enjoying the life God has intended for you to live.

It's amazing how you find people whose hearts were crushed and vandalized but who go back to the same people and situations that did the crushing or vandalizing.

If God took you out of a situation that was not good for you, why would you go back to it? Are you so bonded that you cannot break free from that happening to you all the time?

Many are afraid of ridicule and what people are going say if they see a need to separate themselves from some person or some people, no matter who these may be. If these people truly love you and care for you, they would treat you so. God wants you to live a happy life, a life that is abundant and free.

You have to come to the realization that you have to love yourself.

I am always of the view that it is not God's will for us to live in a damaging way. We are to be experiencing heaven on earth.

Let go of that tormented life; enjoy peace of mind. Or would you rather die unhappy and with a heart full of grief? It's not worth it! Jesus came so that we may have life and that more abundantly!

Do Not Give Up.
Wait on God

Only be thou strong and very courageous, that thou
mayest observe to do according to all the law, which
Moses my servant commanded thee: turn not from
it to the right hand or to the left, that thou mayest
prosper withersoever thou goest. (Joshua 1:7)

*T*onight I want to encourage you. It really doesn't matter on
what side of the tracks you were born; the seed of greatness was
deposited in you before the foundation of the world. It is time for you
to cross over into your God-ordained space in the universe. You were
created for success.

You need to change your perspective on life. You have allowed
yourself to conform to the world around you. When you were growing
up, just because you did not see the silver spoon does not mean that it
did not exist.

One way to stifle success in your life is to think that opportunities
are only for the "lucky ones". There are too many people trapped within
the mindset that success is for the other person, not for them. I want

you to know that in spite of what is happening in your life right now, it is time for you to focus on the truth of God.

Never be so impatient with what God is doing in your life that you desire to run back to old familiar places. The journey of life is never easy, but it is amazing. Success is not about being lucky. It is about the work that you do to achieve it. The only road that matters is the road that leads you to your prosperity. You have spent enough time on the bench of life. It is time to insert yourself into the starting line-up.

In this season, you have to be determined never to quit. The Enemy is not aware that you are constantly sowing good seeds into your own life. The key is not to allow yourself to be tempted or taunted by the Enemy. As your seed of success is being germinated, wait on God and His divine wisdom.

Do not give up. Wait on God!

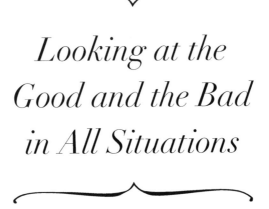

Looking at the Good and the Bad in All Situations

Whilst meditating, I begin to reflect on the Covid-19 pandemic. I also begin to reflect on all that's going on around us.

We serve a God who is awesome and who causes things to happen to get us to where we all need to go. Many of us had dreams, aspirations, gifts, and so forth but never ventured to activate what was in us. God blew our minds by shutting down the whole world, shutting us inside. Whilst inside, many of us began to reflect on life and to do things that they weren't doing before this pandemic started.

Today, I see so many young people who have started their own businesses or, of those who already had a business, extending their services in many unique and creative ways. Many people were given gifts at birth. I see prayer warriors, mouthpieces of God, who came forth in this pandemic.

On the flip side, many people are hurting without jobs, without the money to pay their bills and buy food for their families, and because of this they are forced to trust God to provide for their needs. Many people who had hearts of compassion came forth and are still coming forth to help feed the needy and assist those who are suffering financially.

Assessing this season, I see that God has a way to get us where we need to be in life. It may seem hard for some as some are afraid to come forth in their callings and aspirations.

The Word of God cannot lie. God's ways are not like our ways, and His thoughts are not like our thoughts. If we had continued on with our normal lives, many of us would not have gotten to where we are today. This should cause us to trust God in every season and in any situation in our lives. We serve a faithful God, a God who is trustworthy. I love God, and I thank Him, and I rejoice with everyone whom God has blessed and continues to bless during this pandemic. I'm trusting Him to continue providing for those in need. Trust God and trust His timing.

A Change Is
Going to Come

*M*any people are at a major crossroads in their lives. If you are not actively seeking or creating opportunities for yourself, it is possible that you could get left behind. One of the dangers of not moving when God speaks is that you may find yourself more and more behind the eight ball. The average person is afraid to take on new challenges because it could expose a weakness in their ability to perform the job.

I've come to realize it's all about the decisions we make, and the decisions get tougher to make when the risks seem greater. In order to get what we want, sometimes we are going to have to go against the grain and risk it all. What it took to get the job done last year will not work in this season. It is time to reflect on our actions so that we can avoid the headaches of the past and prevent ourselves from going around in circles. We all make mistakes and poor decisions that we later regret. On the other hand, sometimes a person makes a mistake in life, and even though he or she has paid the price for it and has made a turnaround and tried to live a better life, other people have made it so that person never lives down what he or she did, and as a result, he or she ends up stuck. But aren't you glad that God is not like humankind? He forgives us and gives us a second chance.

The Holy Spirit will come to your rescue and prevent the mistakes of the past from stopping God's manifested blessings in your life. God has a set time for when He is going to dispatch His angels to speak into your life. When these angels appear, it is a sign that the times are changing. Something different is about happen for you, and God does not want you unprepared.

Let me implore you not to waste your time going back to the experiences that have caused you the most pain. God is bringing you into a season of your life where nothing will have any effect on the blessings that are being poured upon you. After you rest, go out on this day, let go, and let God do what He is going to do in your life.

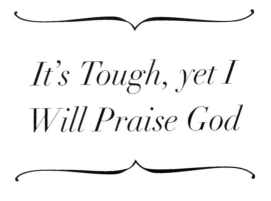

It's Tough, yet I Will Praise God

I will bless the Lord at all times: His praise shall continually be in my mouth. (Psalm 34:1)

Rejoice evermore. Pray without ceasing. In everything give thanks: for this is the will of God in Christ Jesus concerning you. (1 Thessalonians 5:16–18)

All of us have lived lives that have afforded us a few scars, but more importantly the scars have taught many of us valuable lessons. Perhaps the most rewarding of these concerns the phenomenal, life-changing power of praising God whilst we are in the pit of despair and hopelessness.

In this season in which we are living, it is truly a challenge to live our lives in the praise zone. Our scripture verses are easy to read but hard to live! Why? Because life is a struggle. Every day as believers in Jesus Christ, we contend with our fleshly selves, a godless culture, and Satan's attacks. If we are going to live in the praise zone, then we had better be ready to praise God in the tough times. We must learn about tough praise.

There's a song (I don't know if you know it) that says, "When you're up against a struggle that shatters all your dreams, and your hope's been cruelly crushed by Satan's manifested scheme, and you feel the urge within you to submit to earthly fears, don't let the faith you're standing in seem to disappear."

Praise the Lord! He can work through those who praise Him. Praise the Lord! For our God inhabits praise. Praise the Lord! For the chains that seem to bind you serve only to remind you that they drop powerless behind you when you praise Him.

When we all first got saved, we were living on cloud nine; we felt free, and all we had on our minds was Jesus. We all began to feel very holy and as if there was nothing in this world that could make us feel down. Everything seemed perfect. Then one day when life and its circumstance took a turn and the Enemy began to paint a gloomy picture, all that joy unspeakable and full of glory went out of the door. Most of the time, saints fold and become discouraged. If we are not careful, we end up dropping out of the race. And then a bad attitude sets in about our circumstances, and we are left depressed. But I am here to encourage you that no matter what bad circumstance you may find yourself in, no matter how dark your pit may be, every dark cloud has a silver lining. You need to hold your head up high and tell the Devil, "What you may be trying to use to devastate me, God is using to elevate me." So right now, even though it's tough, you should praise God!

The hardest time to truly praise God is when you are going through a tough spot. But saints of God know that this is when we need to give God praise. Praise is a powerful weapon. You may be saying, "That is easier said than done. When I am caught up to my neck in trials and despair, I don't feel like praising God. Pastor, don't you see what I am dealing with? How do you expect me to put on a happy face?" But you can put on a happy face. You see, praise confuses the Enemy. When he expects you to fold up in a chair and throw in the towel, let him see you praising your God, who is worthy of being praised, who is greater than any circumstance you might be faced with.

Anyone can praise the Lord when things are good. But what do you do when you are in a pit? A pit is the point where you reach full recognition of your situation, a stage where you face your powerlessness to overcome the mess in which you sometimes find yourself. Those are the times when you might not hear the sound, because the hurt is so bad; you might not hear a sound because you feel as if you are going to lose your mind. But in spite of the pit, you can move your lips and give Him lip-synced praise. It comes from the human heart and goes to the ears of God. Hallelujah! Are you in a pit today? Whilst there, you can truly get a clear idea of how awesome your God is when you give Him praise. Give God praise!

In the Bible there are many examples of people who said, "It's tough, yet I will praise God."

Our first example is Job. He had a tough time in giving praise. Job experienced life at its worst. Have you ever said, "Things can't get any worse," and they do? Well, we all know the story of Job is the ultimate "It can get worse" story! In a short period of time, Job lost everything that he treasured. He was a wealthy man. In those days, wealth was measured by servants, cattle, and livestock. Job lost it all to thieves and fires. More important to Job, who was a godly man, were his relationships. He loved his children and family. Job's precious family was taken by a series of tragic events. We often hear it said that as long as we have our health, we have everything. Guess what? Job lost his health. Most important of all, Job lost his reputation, his standing in the community.

Job's three friends showed up to cross-examine him in order to discover what had warranted such calamity. To his three friends, the equation was simple enough. God blesses those who do good and curses those who do bad! Good things happen to good people, and bad things happen to bad people. Obviously their friend Job was hiding something from them. Job clung to his innocence and righteousness, but the suspicion of wrongdoing amongst his friends and his community was obvious.

Job hit bottom, cursing the day he was born. We see Job's humanity and weakness throughout the book. If this was a test from God (and it was), then Job did not get everything right, but there was one thing he did manage to do. Job kept his relationship with the Lord unspoiled. When experiencing life at its worst, Job praised the Lord.

Job 1:20–22 says, "Then Job arose, and rent his mantle, and shaved his head, and fell down upon the ground, and worshipped, and said, Naked came I out of my mother's womb, and naked shall I return thither: the Lord gave, and the Lord hath taken away; blessed be the name of the Lord. In all this Job sinned not, nor charged God foolishly." Job asked the question, "Who am I to take the good from God's hand and not receive the bad?" Instead of asking, "Why me?" Job asked, "Why not me?" Job ended up praying for his friends who had hurt him, and he never stopped praising the Lord.

Are you in a pit? Though it's tough, you should still praise God.

Another example is David, who also had a tough praise testimony. David faced the terror of a king made crazy by jealousy and hatred. David spent years as a young man running from a madman. David had the promise of greatness on his life, and it was because of that promise that Saul was jealous of him and hated him. Not everyone was influenced by King Saul, however. There were plenty who believed in David's future and were willing to follow him to the ends of the earth.

In 1 Samuel 30, David takes refuge in a place called Ziklag. One day whilst he and his warriors were away, the Amalekites took advantage of his absence and raided Ziklag, taking spoil, including family members. Upon returning, David and company were overcome by the loss. But then a strange thing happened. Even though David suffered the loss of family in the raid (including his two wives), his fellow comrades turned on him in vengeance, blaming him for their troubles. It is one thing to take the unjust anger of a mad king, but it is another thing to suffer at the hands of your friends, especially when you are grieving over your own loss! Those closest to you can say some very hurtful things when they themselves are hurting. Be careful what you say when you are in the midst of pain and suffering. Words hurt and are remembered!

What a difficult situation. Where do you turn? David turned to the Lord. First Samuel 30:6 says, "And David was greatly distressed; for the people spake of stoning him, because the soul of all the people was grieved, every man for his sons and for his daughters: but David encouraged himself in the Lord his God." David could have acted in kind towards the Lord. After all, it was the Lord through the prophet Samuel who had visited his father's home that day and anointed him as the next king of Israel. He had been content to shepherd his father's sheep. It was God who had transformed his pastoral life into a war zone! But instead of turning from God, David took refuge in God. Just what David said to God is hidden from us. All we know is that David was encouraged in his conversation with the Lord. David chose to live in the praise zone! Though things are tough, yet I will praise God.

Another example for us is of Paul and Silas, who were imprisoned and beaten for fulfilling God's commandment and call upon their lives. We have all heard the story of the jailhouse rock. As Paul and Silas were in Philippi, they encountered a possessed slave girl who was being used by her owners for profit. When Paul grew irritated by her incessant cries, he cast the demonic spirit out of her in the name of Jesus.

This good deed brought severe persecution upon Paul and Silas, who were soon beaten, cast into prison, and placed in stocks. Don't you know that there are saints of God who suffer for fulfilling the call of God on their lives? Now what do you do? When those circumstances arise, you have one of two choices to make: either praise God and continue on walking in your calling, or throw in the towel because you don't want to suffer being talked about, being pulled down, and the like. Now, Paul and Silas had every right to throw a pity party, but instead they threw a praise party! Acts 16:23–25 reads, "And when they had laid many stripes upon them, they cast them into prison, charging the jailor to keep them safely: Who, having received such a charge, thrust them into the inner prison, and made their feet fast in the stocks. And at midnight Paul and Silas prayed, and sang praises unto God: and the prisoners heard them."

Here we learn that praise is warfare. Don't you love that phrase in verse 25, "And at midnight" or "But at midnight"? They were having their midnight experience whilst doing the work of Christ. Satan was having his way, and having his day, with these faithful servants of the Lord, but at midnight, the tide began to turn. When did it turn? It turned when Paul and Silas entered the praise zone!

When things looked the darkest, in a spirit of victory, as God's overcomers, Paul and Silas chose to reflect on who they were in Christ. They began to sing praises to God, right there in prison. Praise is a powerful force against the Enemy because God inhabits the praises of His people. God showed up and that jailhouse began to rock!

Instead of them saying to themselves, *Hey, I'm finished with this tough spot. The cost is too great for me,* they lifted up their voices in praise unto their God and the bars were loosed, the shackles fell off, and the doors flew open. God came off His throne and gave them a standing ovation. I heard one preacher say that as their praises reached the throne, God begin to tap His feet and a great earthquake took place in the prison where His servants were. They gave God an earthquake of praise that night.

Something happens when we praise God, especially when we are going through a really tough time. When we choose to enter the praise zone, no matter what the circumstance, God tears down the walls of the prison built up around us and loosens the shackles of doubt and fear. Praise God at the midnight hour! No matter how you feel, no matter deep your pit may be, God is worthy of your praise. God always responds to the praises of His people.

You have to make up in your mind that you will not allow circumstances to kill your praise. You see, the Devil has a contract out on your praise, but nothing can kill that which God wants to live.

This is what you need to do to get your praise on: every now and then, you need to have a flashback and testify. You see, testimonies are connected to flashbacks, and flashbacks are connected to praise. Every now and then, God wants you to look back on what He has brought you out of, what He has brought you through. You should have been dead, sleeping in your grave. You could have been in a mental institution or laid up in a hospital. You might have had no job, but your bills were not due, and you had food on your table and clothes on your back. You can testify that if it had not been for the Lord being at your side, things would have turned out much worse for you. Flashback, flashback, flashback—give Him flashback praise!

If God didn't bring you out of anything, you can just sit there, but if you can say it was only God who delivered you, I want you to offer three types of praise: coulda praise, woulda praise, and shoulda praise. You ought to praise God for what coulda happened but didn't, what woulda happened but didn't, and what shoulda happened but didn't.

When tough times come, and they always do, we have a choice. We can choose to dwell in the darkness and despair, becoming angry or bitter, or we can choose to live in the praise zone. Are we going to listen to the voice of our flesh or to the voice of God's Holy Word and Spirit? Will we use our minds to review the injustice, the pain, and the suffering in our lives, or will we use our minds to recall God's promises and our changeless position in Christ? Will we open our mouths in complaint or in praise?

Where is your praise? You may be in a pit, but praise God. The power of praise in the pit is that it breaks down the barriers in your heart and mind that limit who God is and what you believe about Him. Praising in the pit edifies God; it allows you to recognize Him as the source of provision in your life. He is your El Shaddai, the God who is more than enough. He is a loving God, and there is nothing sweeter to Him than the sound of praise from one of His children. You may be feeling low in spirit—but praise God! You've got to say to say to yourself, *In spite of what I may be going through, in spite of what it looks like, and though it is tough, I will praise God!*

In choosing praise, we turn our thoughts away from the pain and problems at hand to consider all God that has promised to us. In 2 Corinthians 4, the apostle Paul verbalizes this choice to turn our hearts and minds towards praise. Listen to him in 2 Corinthians 4:8–9, where he says, "We are troubled on every side, yet not distressed; we are perplexed, but not in despair; persecuted, but not forsaken;

cast down, but not destroyed." Do you see the conscious choice Paul makes in these verses? It is not that he ignores his present situation; he simply chooses not to live at that address! Hallelujah! Somebody give God some praise.

No matter what you may be going through or may go through, may you continue to praise God.

This life will soon be over. Jesus is coming soon. Soon we will be done with troubles and trials. Give the Lord praise!

Give Me Grace That I Will Make It After All

*I*heard a sermon preached on the topic "Give Me Grace That I Will Make It After All". It was very inspiring, encouraging, and challenging.

This day and time we are living in is a hard one, a time when the Enemy sets out to discourage us, dampen our spirits, and cause us to want give up on God.

When God has delivered you from the opinions of people and has delivered you from your shortcomings, and when you are focused and happy in God, I can guarantee you that the Devil will try you. But you have to remained focused and keep your eyes upward, on God, because if you listen to what the Enemy may try to whisper in your ear, trying to make you think you are not who God says you are, you will end up in the same state that you were in before.

Serve the Devil notice that no matter what he tries to do or whomever he tries to use to discourage you, he has lost, because greater is He who is in you than he that is in the world.

This is the time to stay focused with your heart and mind stayed on God. #iamdeterminedtoholdouttothend

Gifts

*I*magine waking up on Christmas morning and seeing a pile of presents under the tree but never opening them. Imagine that your friends and family spent a lot of money on you, buying you things you need and desire but could never afford.

Imagine that you even know what is inside those packages but you just decided to let them sit under the tree day in and day out, year after year. After all, now you have what you've always dreamed of. You own whatever is in those boxes. If anyone were to ask, you'd say, "Yes, I have that." But it wouldn't do you any good. You would never be able to use those gifts unless you took the time to unwrap those packages.

Many have unwrapped gifts in their lives and are afraid to open them because of fear, because they dread what others would say, or because they think it's not worth it, that no one will accept what they have to offer.

People today are very selective in terms of whom they will accept and support. This tends to cause a lot of people not to use the gifts that are within them. As result of this, many people who would otherwise be blessed through such individuals are not receiving the joy, deliverance, and so forth that they need.

Friend, it's the same way with God. He wants you to have an abundant life. His gifts are all right there for you, wrapped up in the

Word of God. You open His gift by meditating on His Word, obeying His commands, and declaring His Word with your mouth.

Tonight, I encourage you to unwrap your gifts! Don't let a single present sit under the tree any longer. Jesus paid a precious price so you could have both eternal life and abundant life. Unwrap your gifts and live in His fullness.

As you go to sleep tonight, ask God to help you to receive every good and perfect promise He has for you. Choose to take a step of faith to activate His Word in your life. Let Him teach you by His Spirit, so you may walk and live according to His precepts. Have a blessed sweet sleep!

Delayed but Not Denied

After this there was a feast of the Jews; and Jesus went
up to Jerusalem. Now there is at Jerusalem by the
sheep market a pool, which is called in the Hebrew
tongue Bethesda, having five porches. In these lay
a great multitude of impotent folk, of blind, halt,
withered, waiting for the moving of the water. For
an angel went down at a certain season into the pool,
and troubled the water: whosoever then first after the
troubling of the water stepped in was made whole of
whatsoever disease he had. And a certain man was
there, which had an infirmity thirty and eight years.
When Jesus saw him lie, and knew that he had been
now a long time in that case, he saith unto him, Wilt
thou be made whole? The impotent man answered
him, Sir, I have no man, when the water is troubled, to
put me into the pool: but while I am coming, another
steppeth down before me. Jesus saith unto him, Rise,
take up thy bed, and walk. And immediately the man
was made whole, and took up his bed, and walked:
and on the same day was the sabbath. (John 5:1–9)

*I*n this season in which we are living; a time when we as human beings want everything instantly; a season of the microwave; a time when we want things done yesterday, so to speak, I truly believe that the only thing that will see us through these last days is our faith in God. If it weren't for our faith in God, none of us would be here. But God is calling us to greater faith. God wants us to exercise our faith and take it to new levels.

What is faith? Faith is being sure of what we hope for and certain of what we don't see. I love the promise from Hebrews 11:1 that tells us that even when we do not know or see all things that have been promised to us; when we have prayed for days, years, months, or even years for a specific breakthrough and it has not yet come; when circumstances in our lives are going the exact opposite direction we would prefer; and when we are being pressed on every side, we can put our trust in our Lord and Saviour Jesus Christ and expect that He is going to prove Himself faithful on our behalf.

We all have days when we are filled with faith and days when we wonder how we are going to make it. There are times we are certain in our standing, and then we feel the weight of the burden we are carrying in our place of waiting for breakthrough and deliverance, knowing that He is the only one who can truly deliver us and see us through. But the beauty of the Lord is that He never wastes any season of our lives. He always works all things in our lives for good if we allow Him.

So no matter what you may be waiting on in your life, no matter what your request is to God, I want to assure you that He is going to come through for you. He may not come when you want Him, but He will always arrive right on time. Don't give up. Your breakthrough is right around the corner. Your request is about to be answered.

Go to bed with the assurance that what you are awaiting is right around the corner. Don't allow anxiety to rule your heart and mind. God is on time. As you go to sleep tonight, turn your worries over to Him and have a blessed, restful night.

It's Morning

After the Sabbath, at dawn on the first day of the week, Mary Magdalene and the other Mary went to see the tomb. (Matthew 28:1)

*T*he Christian world celebrates what is called Easter. Easter is said to be a pagan holiday, where folks do not focus on what Christians focus on. Instead they focus on the Easter eggs, the Easter Bunny, etc. To the believer in Christ, our focus is on the death, burial, and resurrection of our Lord and Saviour Jesus Christ, which gives us hope in the face of the unfairness of the world. It gives us strength and courage in every situation that we face. And in this day and time in which we are living, we need strength and courage. I need it. The account of the Easter story is such good news for us as believers. This morning church I want to show how the Resurrection of our Lord validates every promise Jesus ever made. It is the good news that gives hope, light, and encouragement when everything else looks bleak.

We all need to give praise to a God who moved the stone that day and a God who can still move the stones out of our lives today. The great message of Easter is that if Jesus Christ was powerful enough to move the stone and overcome the grave, then He is powerful enough to move the stones that are blocking our lives.

Looking at what happened to our Lord and Saviour and what He had to face on the cross and leading up to His resurrection, we can use this to help us get from we are to where God wants us to be in Him. You see, we go through persecutions, scourging, being laughed at, and being scorned, and for some of us, even our character/name gets crucified. Some people even bury us and put a stone at the tombs of our lives and seal it to keep us down. But I want to tell you that just as Jesus rose from the dead, we too can rise up out of whatever grave we may be in. I want to tell you that this is a new season, a new day. Today can mark a new chapter in your life, but you have to realize it's a new morning. It is a new day in your life because Jesus is alive.

Rest in Him

*T*his life sometimes causes us a lot of grief, pain, disappointment, and oppression. These things arise from what we are faced with in our lives.

So many are going to sleep tonight hurting over a lost child; the death of a loved one; not knowing where the next meal is coming from for their kids; oppression on the job with no one to go to for representation; molestation; domestic violence; or a heart that is heavy with the issues of life.

During this season in life, if you're in any of these situations, know that there is a place of quiet rest that is near to the heart of God. Jesus tells us in the Bible, "Cast all your cares on Me because I care for you." We can rest assured that if there's no one else there for us, God is!

These are the days when the hearts of men and women will be failing because of the cares of this life. Now is the time to turn your worries and cares into prayers. This is a hard world we're living in, but you have to make up your mind whether you're going to be weak or be strong. I implore you to rest in God and be strong.

There are some things in life we have no control over, and therefore there's no need to stress over such things. Life is fragile. Life is short. God wants us to experience heaven on earth. We must trust the process and let Him do the work.

I can assure you who are reading this that God will never fail you, but you need to trust Him. God is a provider, a problem fixer, a mind regulator, and a burden-bearer.

Rest tonight in God. Cast all you cares on Him, my friend. He cares deeply for you. No one else in the world loves you and cares for you more than God does.

Have a restful night. Allow His Spirit to minister to you in your dreams and visions. Be blessed.

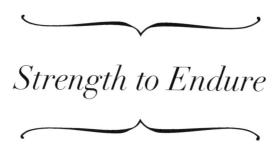

Strength to Endure

*D*uring a long race, it's easy to get discouraged. But what most runners know is that being familiar with the course helps them to keep up momentum and motivation. When you know what to expect, you're able to pace yourself and not get discouraged when the road seems endless.

God doesn't map out for us the exact course of our lives. But there are some things we can know without a shadow of a doubt. We know troubles will come. We know that God will never abandon us. We know that He has good plans for us. And we know that He will ultimately overcome evil in the world. That knowledge and faith helps us persevere when the going gets tough and the race gets long. We can pray and ask God to give us greater confidence in Him so that we might persevere in the race of life.

So no matter what may be weighing you down tonight, please know that God will give you the strength to endure and to come through as pure gold, victoriously. Have a good night's rest as you give all your problems over to the Great I Am, who never sleeps or slumbers and who is always working on your behalf. Have a blessed night!

You Ain't Seen Nothing Yet

But as it is written, Eye hath not seen, nor ear heard, neither have entered into the heart of man, the things which God hath prepared for them that love him. (1 Corinthians 2:9)

You cannot look at a person's shoes and judge where he or she is in life. An old, worn-out shoe can only tell you about the miles a person has travelled, but never his or her life story. It amazes me how people can look at a person and size him or her up by what they see, without knowing anything about the individual.

Many people are dealt what could appear to be a bad hand in life. There are times in life when your outward appearance will not match your inward convictions. However, the question is, how do you handle that hand when it shows up in your life?

In this journey of life, I have learned that a person who is not operating in God-consciousness will always misread or misjudge a situation. It is easy to think that wrong is right when living in a dysfunctional environment. The Enemy would love to use the people around you to destroy you. That is why it is imperative that you *know* who you are in the eyes of God.

You may have spent the majority of your life living in someone else's world, even as far back as a child. But I hear the Spirit of the Lord saying, "You stayed true to yourself and did not allow the negative words that you were hearing to stop you from believing in God's plan for your life. You never allowed what others saw as a lack to take control of your self-esteem. You refused to manifest other people's negative opinions of you. There is so much more to your life. You ain't seen nothing yet!"

Believe it or not, the world has not seen anything yet. Your life is about to tell a story that only God could have written. The Enemy's biggest problem with you is that you refuse to play his game. You have the power and the determination to make things happen according to what you desire. Your ability to take a negative situation and reverse it for your good is masterful. Place your hand over your heart and declare to yourself, "You ain't seen nothing yet!" Have a blessed night!

Let It Go and Tell Your Story

*M*any people ask and wonder, "What is the secret to being happy? Is there a formula for everlasting happiness?" One fact is true— the inability to forgive or the unwillingness to forget what happened on the road of disappointment can lead to sleepless nights. Everyone knows at least one person (it could be you) who has convinced them, "I cannot let it go."

I've come to realize that if you want your life to change for the better, it is imperative that you let go of whatever is slowing you down. Never let the Enemy convince you that holding on to negative events is a right that you should exercise. When you hold on to grudges, it is impossible to connect with people on a deeper level, which can result in shutting out the very people who care the most about you.

You can be so mad at the world that you refuse to allow the Holy Spirit to use you for the glory of God. Anger towards family members, friends, and colleague could cause you to miss out on some of the greatest blessings coming your way. Trials and tribulations come to strengthen you and make you better. When you embrace what God is doing in your life through the trials and tribulations, it will bring a smile to your face. It is at that moment you realize that God is setting you up for something greater than you could ever imagine.

People will be shocked to hear that you are no longer allowing yourself to stay stuck in depression, sadness, disappointment, or grief. Your level of happiness is determined by your testimony that you were able to walk through the fires of life and still live. The Enemy has tried his best to keep you silent. Living in your happy space upsets him greatly.

Your testimony is the key to your happiness, and it opens the door for your greatness to shine. Let this be a great day to close the doors on past disappointments, anger, frustration, and unforgiveness, and begin telling your testimony about how you overcame and walked through the valley of the shadow of death. Victory is yours! Refuse to allow the pain of life to stop you!

What really matters is that you have made it this far and you refuse to back down. You would be amazed at how many people are walking around with a silent testimony. When a testimony remains silent, the gift of God stays dormant. The Enemy knows that your testimony carries life and freedom.

Tonight before falling asleep, let it go! When the opportunity arises, share your testimony with someone else who needs it. Turn it over to God and have a restful night!

God's Constant Love

So often you hear it being said that this world we are living in is an evil, wicked world. This is said so often because of what people experience in their day-to-day lives. The truth of the matter is that people experience so much hate from others nowadays that it causes one to wonder if there is any love at all in their hearts.

How can we say that we love God, whom we never see, when our hearts are so full of hate and animosity for our brothers and sisters whom we do see? Oftentimes you can feel or sense the animosity flowing from others to you. We live in a cold world, and it's going to get even colder as we are nearing the return of Christ. Can you imagine being hated for doing what is right? Can you imagine being hated for the gospel of Jesus Christ? Can you imagine being ignored as if you don't exist?

Truth be told, the love that Jesus has for us is constant. Jesus's personality doesn't change; He is constant. His love is a love that we all can rely on. He doesn't get tired of us. He doesn't toss us aside when we need Him most. His divine love is always readily available to us. He is not like human beings, who say they love only with their lips. He demonstrates His love for us. The biggest demonstration was when He died on the cross.

So if you've been hated, despised, forsaken, tossed aside, told you are nothing, and told that no one will love you, let me assure you tonight that Jesus loves you and He will never treat you the way human beings treat you. His love is constant; it never changes. Go to sleep being assured of His love for you. Jesus loves you!

Forward Ever

*H*ave you ever found yourself at a place in life where the way forward looks hard, so you want to turn around and go back to the place where you were? You've tried to move forward in your career or a relationship or in your walk with Christ, yet in the process things have gotten harder rather than easier. And you then realize that to continue to move forward is going to require more from you than you want to give.

Going back to what you were rescued from may seem easy, but it will bring regrets.

When we get to a place where the way forward looks difficult, we often tend to take a glance back over our shoulders to see what it is we've left behind. And sometimes we conclude that it's just easier to turn around and go back than it is to continue to struggle to move forward.

Why do we as people turn back? You would think it would be obvious that turning back isn't the way forward. And yet professing Christians do it all the time. But why? Because they come to believe that the past is more promising than the future. When the way forward is hard, sometimes people are tempted to turn back.

When the way forward is difficult, it forces you to live by faith and not by sight. That's why going back is much easier; you know what it is you're returning to. You've been there and done that, as we say. And thus there is no faith required to go back to where you once were.

But listen, when it comes to living the Christian life, turning back isn't the way forward. In fact, turning back is madness; it's first-rate folly. This is what Paul says to the Galatians: What you're doing is ludicrous! Why? Because it won't get you where you want to go!

When the way forward as a Christian is hard, you will start hearing voices calling out to you: "Come back." And you'll start recalling memories of how good life used to be. But don't listen to those voices or look to those memories. Understand when your old attachments are talking to you, and learn to turn a deaf ear to those voices and turn a blind eye to those memories.

On the other hand, train yourself to listen to the voice of God in the pages of scripture and with the ears of faith. Look to the promises of scripture with the eyes of faith; hear what God promises to do for you as a son or daughter; and see all that He has in store for you as an heir of the inheritance through Christ.

What you find when you turn back to the things of your past is perhaps some short-term reward, but in the end you wind up enslaved. This is Paul's first word of warning to the Galatians, and it's a warning to us also: by turning back to the garbage of your past, you won't go forward to the glory God has promised.

Turning back means turning your back on the only One who truly knows you, who is God!

When you turn back, you find, not greater freedom, but great bondage. But that's not the worst thing about turning back. What's worse is this: by turning back to the old attachments of your preconversion past, you wind up turning your back on the only One who can save you.

Turning back isn't the way forward. It won't get you where you want to go; it won't get you where you need to go. The only way to the Promised Land is through the wilderness. That's true for us as a church, and it's true for you as an individual. The way through the wilderness is the appointed path for God's people. There is no other way forward.

Going forward leads you into freedom and life. Going back plunges you into slavery and death. Going forward will lead you into the kingdom of God. Going back will cause you to perish in the wilderness. Going back isn't the way forward. Make up your mind tonight that you will not go back but you will move forward.

Coping with Difficult Seasons

To everything there is a season, and a time to every purpose under the heaven: a time to be born, and a time to die; a time to plant, and a time to pluck up that which is planted; a time to kill, and a time to heal; a time to break down, and a time to build up; a time to weep, and a time to laugh; a time to mourn, and a time to dance; a time to cast away stones, and a time to gather stones together; a time to embrace, and a time to refrain from embracing; a time to get, and a time to lose; a time to keep, and a time to cast away; a time to rend, and a time to sew; a time to keep silence, and a time to speak; a time to love, and a time to hate; a time of war, and a time of peace. (Ecclesiastes 3:1–8)

The natural seasons are winter, spring, summer, and autumn. There are also spiritual seasons in our lives. What spiritual season are you experiencing now? Are you trusting God to help you in the season you are in?

In the lives of all believers, we will face times of great difficulty and times of great joy. We will experience seasons of hard work and seasons of plenty. We will spend seasons on the hilltop, and we will spend time down in the valley. I want to tell you today that God can use each of these seasons of life to teach us something about who He is and how much He loves us.

We may never fully understand what God has planned for us, but our attitude towards life changes when we learn to see good times and bad times as opportunities to grow closer to our heavenly Father.

I'm sure from the time the Covid-19 pandemic began up to now, most can testify that they have grown closer with God.

As we journey through the seasons of life, we will experience many ups and downs. Perhaps in your own life you have experienced the highs and the lows. Maybe right now you are going through something that feels like a ride on a roller coaster. Many who have ridden real roller coasters say that they enjoyed it. Some relay how afraid they were. For me, the couple of times I rode one, I thought I was going to die.

Roller coasters go up and down, make twists and turns, do loops, and take plunges. A ride on a roller coaster is over in a couple of minutes, and maybe for those two minutes you hold on so tight that your hands hurt. Whilst the ride is in motion, you laugh, you scream, you cry, and maybe you struggle to get your breath. Then it's over. You are safe. You disembark from the roller coaster and stand on solid ground again. Then one of two things usually happens: either you head back to the end of the queue so that you can do it again, or you throw up, vowing never again to be so stupid, and move on.

We all experience ups and downs in our lives, some to the extent that we feel like no longer living so we won't have to go through such experiences. But as Christians, as disciples of Jesus, we do not face these times of difficulty on our own—God is with us. His promise to us is that He will never leave us or forsake us.

What spiritual season are you experiencing right now? Do you feel as if you are on roller coaster right now through this pandemic, not knowing how your life is going to be? Are you trusting God to help you in the season you are in?

If we put our trust in God, then whatever we are going through, whatever circumstance or situation we are in, whether we feel that we are deep in a valley of despair or on top of a mountain, in good times or bad times, we can be certain that God is with us.

First Peter 5:7 reminds us that we can bring all our cares, all our worries, all our hopes, all our fears, and all our dreams to God because He cares about us—each and every one of us.

Whatever season you feel you are in, whatever circumstance or situation you are in right now, have you made the time to really pray about it? And if you have prayed about it, were you just on transmit, or did you take the time to pause and listen to God to receive His guidance? That is the type of conversation that you need to have. When you pray, you need to wait and listen to what God is saying.

I've heard many people ask the Lord: Why is there so much injustice in this world? Why is there so much pain? Why do the evil and the wicked seem to prosper so much? Why are victims often treated worse than the criminals? Why do the innocent suffer? Why are You allowing this virus to be so rampant in our land? During these times, I encourage you to trust God. In these times when it seems as if God is not near or is far away from what's going on, trust Him even when you can't trace Him.

I want to encourage you in the following ways:

In the springtime of life, trust God; in the summer of life, trust God; in the autumn of life, trust God; in the winter of life, trust God; in the good times, trust God; in the bad times, trust God.

In the calm before the storm, trust God; when the storm comes, trust God.

In the midst of the storm, trust God; after the storm, trust God.

During times of difficulty you may be going through, be faithful to God. Be steadfast in your faith. Whatever season you are in, have faith.

There are seasons when we will question what God is doing. There are seasons when we will not understand what God is doing. But in every season, we must have faith in God. We must trust Him in every circumstance, in every situation, in every difficulty, and in every blessing. Trust God.

Faith—such a small word for something so important and essential.

I want you to realize that my faith in God is not dependent on your faith in God. Your faith in God is not dependent on my faith in God. Each of us needs to have our own personal faith in God for every season of life.

We must have a living, active faith, a strong faith in God despite the circumstances, despite what the world is experiencing, despite what our country is experiencing, despite what you and I are experiencing right now. We must choose to trust and believe in God. From Romans 8:28, we know that God causes everything to work together for the good of those who love Him and are called according to His purposes.

Despite how you feel, despite your circumstances, your faith in God will sustain you. Our God is sovereign. God is in control, and He is a God who listens and responds to His people.

May God help us to have faith in every season of life. Have a restful night!

Where Is Your Anchor?

Trust in the Lord with all thine heart; and lean not unto thine own understanding. In all thy ways acknowledge him, and he shall direct thy paths. (Proverbs 3:5–6)

*I*f we look around the world today and even in our own society, we can see more than ever the need for our lives and our hopes to be anchored in Jesus, who is the solid Rock. The songwriter penned, "My anchor holds and grips the solid rock. Who is the rock? … This rock is Jesus. He's the one. This rock is Jesus, the only one. … We are to be sure, be very sure, our anchor holds and grips the solid rock."

Many folks are going through hard times in their lives; many are on the verge of giving up. As we look around us, we can see all kinds of things happening right before our eyes. People are dying—the young, the old, and the in-between. Sickness and diseases are on a rampage. People are depressed, oppressed, sick, busted, and disgusted, not knowing whom to turn to. But I am stopping by to let you know today that the only solution to whatever it is you may be faced with is to be anchored in God.

Despite what is going on in your life, I want to remind you that

God knows how to do a miraculous thing. There is nothing too hard for that anchor to do. There is no sickness He can't heal. There is no burden He can't lift. He is the same God who delivered the children of Israel. He is the same God of Shadrach, Meshach, and Abednego, the God of Joseph and Daniel, the same God who healed the blind, healed the man at the pool of Bethesda, raised the dead, and turned water into wine. He is that same God. You need Him as your anchor.

Are you under a storm cloud? Can you see one coming on the horizon? Rather than tying down the boat and securing it on man-made docks, you are to anchor your life in Christ. You do this by spending time with Him. You need to seek God's will in any matter you may be challenged with and let Him have full control of your ship. The only way to survive in the storms of life is by seeking refuge in Him. Psalm 91 says, "He that dwelleth in the secret place of the Most High shall abide." Are you abiding? Are you standing firm on that solid Rock?

Many don't dwell in Christ anymore. Many have turned away to witchcraft, man-made religions. Many are putting their trust in humankind, flesh—but the arm of flesh will fail. Dare not trust your own.

At times in our lives we go through storms that seem to last forever. Our nights of confusion, tossing and turning, sleeplessness and loneliness, pain and brokenness—it seems as if the storm will never pass. Then we reach the place where we feel as if our God has forsaken us. But saints of God, I've come to realize that the Enemy places those thoughts of doubt in our minds to get us to stop anchoring our trust in El Shaddai, the God who is more than enough; to stop holding on to the burden-bearer; to stop anchoring our trust in the sea walker who can calm any storm which we may have in our lives; the One who is a shelter in a time of storm; our Shepherd; our Friend who sticks closer than any brother. I'm talking about Jesus!

Have you ever reached a point when you are just tired of everything in life? Have you ever felt like throwing in the towel and forgetting about everything? Doesn't that sound like the Enemy? You see, he knows just what God has in store for our lives. If we could all see how our end will be and what God has in store for us, we wouldn't feel like giving up. You see, in this life, there is hope for the believer. There is a bright light at the end of any tunnel we may be going through, and we'll be able to see it once we let our small anchor be anchored in the large anchor which is that man from Galilee, who died on the cross for you and me more than two thousand years ago.

Psalm 11:3 tells us, "When the foundations are being destroyed, what can the righteous do?" What do you do when your foundations are destroyed by unexpected circumstances of economic hardship; severe sickness; unjust treatment by authorities; disobedient children; a loved one's death? What would you do if you were tried like Job?

When severe storms beat against the ship of your life, do you have an anchor that steadies your soul? What is this hope you are grasping? Is it your bank account, material things, the promises of politicians? Many people put their hope and trust in people more than in God.

Our anchor of hope is Jesus Himself, who died for our sins and was raised for our justification. The Word says, "We have this hope." It is in the present tense, meaning we have it now, continuously. When we face adversity, we have it; when we go to the doctor and get a bad report, we have it; when we face death, we have it; when our children aren't acting right, we have it; when our loved ones die, we have it. We have this hope! Tell yourself, "I have this hope!"

Printed in the United States
by Baker & Taylor Publisher Services